UNITY BOOKS

FROM THE LIBRARY OF

_____

_____

PROSPERITY'S
TEN
COMMANDMENTS

Also by Georgiana Tree West

Usable Psychology (OP)

PROSPERITY'S TEN COMMANDMENTS

GEORGIANA TREE WEST

Unity Classic Library

unity®
HOUSE

Unity Village, Missouri

Prosperity's Ten Commandments
is a member of the Unity Classic Library.

In its original version, *Prosperity's Ten Commandments* was published by
Theo Gaus' Sons, Inc. in 1944. Copyright © 1944 by Georgiana Tree
West.

The first Unity edition was printed in 1946, and eight editions followed.

To place an order, call the Customer Service Department at
1-800-669-0282 or visit us online at *www.unityonline.org*.

First printing 1946; tenth printing 1996
Second edition, first printing 2005

The New Revised Standard Version is used for
all Bible verses unless otherwise noted.

LIBRARY OF CONGRESS CATALOGING-IN-PUBLICATION DATA
West, Georgiana Tree, b. 1882.
     Prosperity's Ten Commandments / Georgiana Tree West.
        p.   cm. — (Unity classic library)
     ISBN 0-87159-306-8
     1. Unity—Doctrines. 2. Ten commandments. 3. Wealth—
Religious aspects. 4. Success—Religious aspects.
I. Title. II. Series.
BX9890.U505W47   1996
248.4'8997—dc20   96-3228
                                                            CIP

Canada GST R132529033

"Through the process of thought, mind projects its ideas into the realm of form. When the ideas generated in mind are true to the spiritual power that enables us to be, to think, and to act, they appear in the realm of form in ways that make for peace of mind, health of body, and abundant well-being in circumstances."

Georgiana Tree West

EDITOR'S NOTE

Prosperity's Ten Commandments has appeared in a number of different formats since its inception in 1946. First a small-sized hardcover, it evolved into a booklet format that was inexpensive but did not do justice to the importance of the material or the author.

We decided to bring the book back into print as a Unity Classic but to do so required adding additional material to bring the book up in size. We collected all the written material by Georgiana Tree West we could find and read it all, finally deciding upon two pamphlets that provided more of the author's considerable insight into this book's prosperity theme. Both pamphlets were originally published by the Unity Center of Practical Christianity in New York City.

We also chose to include the essay written by Dana Gatlin, author of the ever-popular *God Is the Answer*, as a Foreword. Published in *Unity Magazine* in 1940, this piece is the perfect introduction to Georgiana Tree West, giving testament to her as both woman and minister.

—Michael A. Maday
1996

CONTENTS

FOREWORD

Georgiana Tree West: One With That Light

"Make your ill experiences pay you. If an adversity drives you to seek Truth and to know the One Power that is with you always and that never fails, you are ineffably blessed!"

This was a striking, luminous point in the message gleaned from our interview with Georgiana Tree West. Mrs. West, for many years located at Louisville, Kentucky, is now leader of a Unity center in New York City. She has experienced many and varied vicissitudes, is endowed with mental equipment of a high order, and has a record of unusual spiritual achievement. She states that she first became interested in the Truth teaching because of her desire to get relief from poor health of long standing as well as to find help for her husband, whose financial situation had been adversely affected because of his having to pay her doctor bills.

So it is significant to us, as it was to Mrs. West, that she was impressed by what a Truth teacher said to her at the time she was first seeking aid through spiritual means: "If you ever have to go through hell, make it pay you!" This of course is a paraphrase of the Psalmist's "If I make my bed in Sheol, behold, thou art there." Another high point in Mrs. West's spiritual adventure was when she demonstrated through her own experience the truth of the familiar lines:

"Then give to the world the best you have,
And the best will come back to you."

Our character is largely determined by our environment during childhood's formative years. Georgiana Tree West was born in London, an only child, and she was a lonely child. She came to this country with her parents, who always lived in big cities. She disliked to go to England to visit because she didn't know how to play with her cousins. She liked to read rather than play, was imaginative and introspective, and had too much time alone to read and think. At Sunday school she asked the teacher some very pointed questions about the familiar scriptural incidents, such as the Flood, and was rebuked instead of having her questions answered. However, in her childish mind, Georgiana wasn't much interested because she considered God a big bully and she just didn't like God. Privately she decided that she was through with God, but she had learned to be discreet because "naughty little girls" get punished.

It was an abnormal childhood, Mrs. West admits, and although she attended church and Sunday school, she had no real religious life until she was about fifteen years old. Then she chanced upon Christian Science, and this attracted her questioning, thirsty mind. The principle that God, Spirit, is the living intelligence that underlies the whole formed universe greatly helped her inner queries but brought small comfort. She had to obey cold principle, otherwise—but she kept asking herself, "If this flesh is just one big lie, then why do we strive to keep it, to perpetuate it?" She could not answer the question satisfactorily, no one else did, and eventually the perturbed young seeker gave up her study. She was grateful for the idea that God is divine principle working in immutable law. That at least was a great improvement over the unjust, barbaric, never-explained records of the Scriptures, and further enlightenment was to come to her later.

Then young Georgiana grew up and married, and life became quite a varied, hectic affair. For many years most of her time was spent in mining camps, and she was constantly being uprooted. She learned to ride, shoot, and play poker, acquiring adaptability, which is one of life's biggest lessons. This wife of a mining engineer was always fearlessly ready to face an emergency.

"In Mexico," relates Mrs. West, "one of our carpenters went berserk. His wife ran to me for help, and I corralled the man and put him to bed. Everybody looked to Mr. West and me for help with all kinds of things: weddings, celebrations, amusing and farcical situations, puzzling problems, real tragedies. I had never had any experience to prepare me for all this, but life just precipitated me into it.

"Then I began to be ill. I had three major operations and two babies in six years and succumbed to 'delicate health.' I think my shifting mental state affected my health: some organs did not heal, and I felt very sorry for myself—yes, I wore the martyr's crown and pressed in the thorns! I was always seeing doctors. I went to sleep at night dreading to wake up in the morning.

"Then I got rebellious, which is a good sign! My husband had become interested in constructive thinking and was using it in his business affairs, and he thought it might help my health. But I wasn't very eager. You see, I hated to give up the sympathy I was devoting to myself," says Mrs. West with her humorous, understanding smile. "But I did try, and I began to get a link between constructive thinking on my own part and the 'immutable principle' that I had faintly perceived earlier. I began to live with God as my very own strength and power. 'He within me makes my way perfect, and my body is the temple of the living God,' I had read somewhere.

"I read everything along this line that I could get hold of. It is strange, but at that time I had never heard of Unity. I studied theosophy and Buddhism and decided to live with these ideas until I developed the power to generate only constructive ideas.

I thought much of the tremendous power of the mind, of the forces that work in us as life and law, and I lived with the findings of men like Emerson and Troward.

"However, the application of principle was working in my own organism: as my mind clarified my body improved. I kept mulling over these things. I attended church services regularly just because it was the thing to do, and I knew it was a good habit: it built up my spiritual morale. Our children were sent to a denominational Sunday school. I had never joined a church and looked upon myself as a nonreligious woman. In 1924 my husband's business took him to Louisville. His affairs were in a precarious state: I had made him a poor man with my constant doctor bills. In Louisville, I met a young woman who wanted me to go to the Unity center there, but my husband and I had had some rather unhappy experiences with certain cultists we had met, and we decided we wouldn't get mixed up with any more of those 'queer' people.

"But one Easter I had an uncontrollable urge to go to the Unity service, and my husband and I went. It was held in a small room in the Masonic Building. A woman came out and began speaking, and every word she said was as if I were saying it. It was an unforgettable experience, that clear transfusion of Spirit, with no concepts of the mortal 'self' getting in the way! I was enthralled, uplifted.

"At the close, as the crowd was leaving, the speaker lifted her hand and looked at me. 'Wait, I want to talk to you.'

"She came, and we talked a little; then she asked me to assist her as the Truth center hostess. Of course I was startled, yet just then to accept seemed a quite natural thing to do. I was delighted, I felt so uplifted and *enrapport*, and I enjoyed the work and the wonderful spiritual atmosphere that was so spontaneously evoked. When she later asked me to take charge of the Wednesday morning classes, I demurred because I had had so little preparation. 'Your whole life has been a preparation,' she replied. 'These years of intensive study have prepared you. The Holy Spirit does the work. You and I are only God's instruments attuned to receive Him.'

"Well, she had gone East and was detained there, and I received this telegram: 'Expecting you to be on the platform Sunday morning.' I said to my husband, 'Why, I can't give spiritual leadership—I'm not a religious woman!'

"But I prayed, and I did go on the platform that Sunday morning and presented the lesson. I felt that it was a good lesson, for I was feeling deeply the reality of the spiritual presence. I continued to present the lessons during the speaker's absence. Then one morning after saying the benediction, I had a very strange experience."

Mrs. West hesitated about publishing this experience lest it be misunderstood. Yet a similar experience must come to every Truth seeker before he or she is reborn into full awareness of oneness with God. Mrs. West says that at first she did not grasp just what was taking place:

"Right after speaking the benediction, I felt an ineffable peace pervade my whole being, which was translated into terms of light. Light filled me, was all about me; in the whole universe there was nothing but blessedness and light. This wasn't at all a psychic experience, but something far deeper, wider, and more vital than that. I stood there for some time, forgetful of all else but of being one with that light. When I returned to a sense of my surroundings, I said to an associate, 'Rose, something's happened.' 'It is all right,' Rose replied. 'Everyone went home. They thought you were in a meditation.'

"In a few days when our leader came back from New York, she said she had the conviction that it was time for me to take the leadership of the center. Plans were taking her elsewhere, and although I had not known it, she had been sending out a call for a leader to take her place. It still seemed to me that I had not had sufficient spiritual training for leadership, but she told me that she had singled me out that Easter Sunday when I first attended the services at the center."

Within five months Mrs. West was doing full-time work at the center, and in eleven months she became the leader. From the time "the light" came to her as she stood upon the platform, she devoted herself to prayer, meditation, and study, which under the guidance of Spirit would enable her to carry on the work. After all, the period of her preparation was not brief: for years she had been earnestly exploring the Truth of spiritual discipleship that leads to power. From the moment she accepted her call, she consecrated her mind, heart, and whole life to this spiritual work. Long after the center at Louisville had become one of the most effective Unity groups in the country, she voluntarily came to Unity World Headquarters and took the formal course of training that had been agreed upon by the recently formed conference of Unity center leaders.

Under Mrs. West's leadership, the work at the Louisville center increased steadily. "In four months," she says, "we moved from the little room in the Masonic Temple to quarters in the finest hotel in the city. We were there four years, expanding each year, until we finally moved into our own building, an old Southern mansion of fifteen rooms. Next door the Woman's Club was housed in another old mansion, and they let us use it when we needed more space."

In this building, Mrs. West spent eight happy,

fruitful years. She gained a healthier body through the application of Truth principles; her husband was relieved of the doctor bills; she grew in faith so that she could dispense Truth to others. She was a convincing, potent speaker although she had never had any specific training for public speaking. "I came to know that there is a loving, wise presence within us," she says simply. "I just stand and realize this before going on the platform. God never fails us when we open ourselves to Him."

Faith supported the followers of Truth when the devastating floods came to Louisville a few years ago, and faith safely infolded the lovely old building that housed their center.

"All around us the streets and houses were inundated," says Mrs. West, "but our home of Truth was built on a rise of ground, the high waters were kept away from us, and even the cellar remained dry. Because our rooms were bone dry, we were able to serve as a relief station. Boats went by in the street, the Woman's Club next door was flooded, but even our water pipes did not give way, and we could heat bath water constantly in our basement.

"Our center workers started right in with prayer services at the onset of danger, and these were kept up continuously day and night. For those who put their whole trust in the supreme Power, there was nothing to fear. Of course there were no lights, as the electrical service was out of commission, but we used kerosene lamps.

"In our building was a 'Silence Room,' consecrated once a month, in which there was never any
speech or discussion. Simply to enter this room was
to feel the spiritual Presence. A boy was brought in
by one of the rescue boats. He was so low that no
hope was felt for him, but he had heard of our
silent ministry and so he was put in this quiet
room. The nurses were very busy; cots and nurses
were all over the rest of the house. After a while a
nurse went into the room, for there was no sound
and she thought he was gone. But she found him
peacefully sleeping. In three days he was up, eating.
That room was saturated with the Holy Spirit, and
so much strength went out invisibly that it revital-
ized and restored the boy."

Naturally Mrs. West treasures this center where
she found her capacities for spiritual service, and
her human heart would have urged her to stay. But
her husband's business took him away, and home
ties no longer bound her to Louisville. From Unity
World Headquarters came a call to wider service,
and new leaders had been developed in the
Louisville center. So more than a year ago Mrs.
West went into the field as a lecturer, and she is
now located in New York City as leader of the
Unity Center of Practical Christianity.

There was a need to be filled. "You and the Holy
Spirit can fill it!" encouraged Charles Fillmore.

Mrs. West found that she could. She has proved through varying vicissitudes and in the development of courage, faith, strength, and radiant blessing that she is an instrument attuned to the one saving Power.

—Dana Gatlin
1940

INTRODUCTION

The Ten Commandments are cardinal laws for human society. *Cardo* in Latin means "hinge"; therefore, cardinal laws are those on which other laws depend or hinge. They are fundamental laws because they are the basis or foundation upon which all principles of right action may be built.

The Ten Commandments will continue to serve as a basis of right action for all people at all times and in all ways as the fundamental Truth in each is better understood. As our understanding grows, we are able to see greater meaning in these laws and to make broader application of them. This is what Paul meant by "the fulfilling of the law" (Rom. 13:10).

One way to make broader application of the Ten Commandments in our daily lives is to use them as a basis of action in handling all our financial affairs. This revelation came to me while meditating on hidden values in the Commandments. Out of this revelation, *Prosperity's Ten Commandments* evolved. They go to you with the prayer that they may prove to be of as much value in your life as they have been in the life of the author.

THE FIRST COMMANDMENT

You shall look to no other source but God for your supply.

"You shall have no other gods before me"
—Exodus 20:3

Pilate's question, "What is truth?" (Jn. 18:38), is the cry of every person's soul at some time in his or her existence. Even as Jesus stood silently before Pilate as the revealed answer, so the Christ in everyone silently awaits recognition as the Truth of his or her being.

Truth is the state in which Spirit dwells, a state of perfection that is eternally, creatively active. Truth may be briefly defined as the action of Spirit. As such, it is unlimited in nature and cannot be confined within the restrictions of time or space. In other words, Truth once voiced is true under any circumstances for all eternity.

When Moses delivered the Ten Commandments to the Children of Israel, he voiced the Truth God had revealed to him concerning the relationship of people to their Creator and to their fellows. The Ten Commandments, in the form in which Moses gave them, served as a basis of right action toward God and humanity for the unruly, primitive people that Moses led out of Egyptian bondage. Each commandment is an embodiment of Truth; therefore, the form can be changed to meet the needs of all people, at all times, under all conditions.

Truth is capable of limitless expansion. For this reason, we find the essential Truth embodied in the Ten Commandments to be not only the basis of right spiritual and moral conduct, but also the basis for establishing permanent prosperity.

The first commandment is the very foundation of Christianity: "You shall have no other gods before me." We are to acknowledge no other source of life, love, wisdom, and power than our Creator. Only with this secure foundation can we bring into manifestation our spiritual perfection. In this same commandment, we find the only sound basis for the manifesting of permanent prosperity. It is prosperity's first commandment:

You shall look to no other source but God for your supply.

Our Scriptures fairly teem with exhortations to look to God as the one source of supply. The Old and New Testaments are filled with promises of rich fulfillment of every need for those who acknowledge God's presence and power. David, the shepherd king, voiced the confidence of humanity in a Creator who is able and willing to provide for His creation when he said, "For God alone my soul waits in silence, for my hope is from him" (Ps. 62:5).

Humans have always looked to Deity for their heart's desires. One primitive belief was that of buying the favor of Deity through making gifts and sacrifices. Sacrifice played an important part in many of the earlier forms of religious worship. Since human life was held to be the most precious of all gifts, it too was offered to Deity in propitiation to insure good crops, good hunting, and victory over enemies.

The Hebrews were among the first to introduce the idea that human conduct has something to do with gaining the favor of Deity. They saw Deity as a mighty king, a stern but righteous judge. They conceived the idea that prosperity, health, happiness, and protection were rewards for good conduct meted out by their God—the ruler of heaven and earth. They still saw Deity as a power outside His universe demanding obedience and worship. But all through the Old Testament there are evidences of growing understanding of the relationship between God and humanity. This understanding was a necessary preparation for the revelation of Jesus that God dwells in us, has already provided for our every need, and awaits only our expression of trust in God and our acceptance of God's bountiful blessings to deliver them into our lives.

Both the Old and the New Testaments are filled with promises of God revealed through spiritually illumined minds. There is the promise in the book of Job, "Agree with God, and be at peace; in this way good will come to you" (Job 22:21). Again in Deuteronomy, we have the promise, "But remember the Lord your God, for it is he who gives you power to get wealth" (Deut. 8:18). And in Psalms, we find, "When you open your hand, they are filled with good things" (Ps. 104:28). All the promises are summed up in Jesus' statement, "Do not be afraid, little flock, for it is your Father's good pleasure to give you the kingdom" (Lk. 12:32).

The history of poverty in the race of humankind and in the lives of individuals can be directly traced to a lack of faith in God as the source of all supply. With faith in God, we fear no evil, and poverty is an evil. It is the cause of sin and misery and fills our jails and our hospitals to overflowing. Jesus said that a tree is known by its fruits. The tree of poverty bears the fruit of theft, unhappiness, and disease. Its seeds are evil; all that they produce is misery and desperation.

It is of no use to try to idealize poverty. The idea that there are spiritual benefits accruing from it made possible the appalling condition of the masses during the Middle Ages. The people of that time suffered under mental inertia, passivity of mind that accepted their woeful condition because a corrupt clergy, working hand in glove with the state, led them to believe that those who bowed under the yoke and served the church and the ruling classes faithfully laid up treasure in heaven. They were taught that heaven was a place to which they went when they died, but Jesus taught that heaven is the all-embracing harmony of the kingdom of God within every person. He taught that we store up treasure in our own ever-present heaven, "where neither moth nor rust consumes and where thieves do not break in and steal" (Mt. 6:20). This stored-up treasure is our consciousness or awareness of the spiritual richness within us that supplies our every need according to our faith. Jesus said, "It is your Father's good pleasure to give you the kingdom" (Lk. 12:32); in other words, it is God's goodwill to deliver the riches of the kingdom as the fulfillment of every good and just need if we will but trust and accept.

The fact that we sometimes learn much-needed lessons through unhappy experiences such as illness or poverty does not make them right. The lesson is the hidden good in them that proves Omnipresence—that we can never be separated from God and God's good. The Psalmist said, "If I make my bed in Sheol, you are there" (Ps. 139:8). The wretched experience is not a true outpicturing of the invisible Presence: it is our own warped mental

image taking form. Poverty is a form of hell caused
by blindness to God's good. Like the ostrich, we
often bury our heads in the sand of poverty and
cannot see the riches of the Father's kingdom
within ourselves and all around us.

When Jesus revealed God as Spirit, living intelligence, he made it easier for us to understand God's
omnipresence as a creative power instantly ready to
respond to the call of faith, limitless supply ever
seeking expression in form. All growth in nature
illustrates the way potential power expands into
myriads of forms under the right conditions. An
acorn has all the potentialities of the mighty oak,
but its outer shell and inner meat show no evidence
of the tree that is to be. However, the tree is there
as potential power, power that remains static until
the right conditions of moisture, heat, and nourishment are provided. Within us there is almighty
power, the power that God has given us, in which
lies the potentiality of all the good our hearts can
ever desire. This power is static until brought forth
into expression by conditions furnished by mind.
Nourished by faith, it expresses itself in forms
shaped by thoughts.

The first step, then, in manifesting supply is to
establish faith in omnipresent spiritual substance
as the source of all that is. We reason after this
fashion: God is my supply. God is spiritual substance everywhere present. Therefore, my supply is

everywhere present. My acknowledgment of God's omnipresent, spiritual substance delivers it into my life as the fulfillment of my needs.

Jesus summed this up very simply in his instructions concerning prayer. He told us that we are first to seek (acknowledge) the presence of God, and then ask, believing that we receive (accept) the good desired. Such prayer is obeying prosperity's first commandment and looking to God as the only source of supply. This was the way he taught the disciples to pray. First seek God's presence, "Our Father in heaven" (Mt. 6:9), and then ask for the need of the day, "Give us this day our daily bread" (Mt. 6:11). Seven short, simple words; no begging, no beseeching; just a cup of faith lifted to the infinite Good to be filled to overflowing. Countless numbers use this prayer daily, but it fulfills its purpose only when the heart is filled with faith in God's presence and in God's infinite creative power ready and waiting to be transformed into the desire of the heart. The words themselves are a "coverall" designed to cover every possible need of mind and body. Bread, in the language of mysticism, is substance, the invisible energy of Divine Mind, which is the essence of all form. When we say, "Give us this day our daily bread," we are asking of God, "Give us all that we need of Thy spiritual substance in whatever form we need it this day."

We are asking for more of God's life as health

and strength, more of God's love as peace and happiness, more of God's wisdom and power as success and prosperity. When we fail to receive "our daily bread," it is because we cannot receive God's good while we are thinking in terms contrary to that good. If we want a beautiful home, we do not think of going into the slums to look for it; if we want God's good, we must stop "slumming" in mind. It is a law of mind that whatever is held in mind eventually must appear in form. If we pray for one thing but think another, it is the thing we think about that is going to shape itself in our daily lives. When we think confidently about what we have asked in prayer, nothing can keep it from us.

We know that God is Divine Mind, living intelligence. We can say of ourselves: *I, too, am a living intelligence; I am mind and therefore creative of nature. I have a body that is the product of my mind and I live in circumstances that are also the product of my mind.* When we pray, "Give us this day our daily bread," and then see ourselves as poor and unsuccessful, we set up a contradiction in mind that is bound to result in chaotic conditions of lack and limitation. On the other hand, when we accept our daily bread from our Father with the unquestioning faith of a little child and then discipline our minds to think joyfully of God's bounty instead of our fears and worries, we are bound to prosper.

Lack of vision limits our prosperity. We

mistakenly see our business, our employer, our investments, or some individual who pays our bills as the source of our supply. If the job, the investment, or the individual fails us, we are sunk in despair, feeling that the source of our prosperity is cut off. What we need to realize is that all material avenues of supply are merely the pay clerks of God. If an individual is working for a reliable firm and the pay clerk who gives the individual his or her envelope each week makes a mistake or absconds, the individual is not disturbed, because he or she knows that the firm will make good.

The firm of God and Us, Inc., never fails. No matter what the junior partner does, the senior Partner always makes good. Pay clerks may come and go, but God's infinite resources can always be depended on to become manifest through some new channel. We frequently hear the expression "pay on demand" used in the business world. We need to learn that God always pays on demand— the demand of faith. When any human channel of supply fails, we have only to remember that the source of supply will continue to fill our needs through some other channel when we send out our call of faith.

Many people limit their prosperity by the bondage in which they hold others. They feel that they are poor because people do not pay them what they owe them. They look to their debtors rather than to God as the source of supply. When they can enlarge their vision and see that prosperity comes from God only, they will have a very different attitude toward debtors. They will be able to say with conviction: *You are not the source of my supply. I look only to God for my prosperity. God has innumerable channels through which supply comes into my life. You are one of the channels of abundance for me.*

This new vision lifts both the individual and the debtor out of the bondage of false belief. The idea of debtor no longer exists. It is supplanted by the realization that all God's children are partakers of God's bounty and are channels through which that bounty flows to others. Substituting this new clarified thought for the old limited one is forgiving the debtor as we are instructed to do in the Lord's Prayer.

When we look to God alone as the source of our supply, there is no limit to the wealth of good things that can be manifested in our lives. God never limits us. We limit ourselves by filling our minds with fears, doubts, worries, and false beliefs that prevent us from accepting our divine heritage of abundant good. Jesus taught us to find in nature illustrations of God's action in our own lives. Everywhere in nature we find lush abundance. Constantly recurring cycles of growth, blossoming, and fruitage bear witness to the fact that there truly is plenty of substance constantly manifesting through the operation of natural law. This same spiritual substance also constantly manifests through mental law. All the marvels of modern civilization bear mute testimony that limitless, omnipresent, spiritual substance is ever ready to manifest in form according to the ideas in our minds.

Imagine yourself walking down Fifth Avenue in New York. Try to see it as it was five hundred years ago, a part of a wooded island. A deer might have been grazing where the Empire State Building now stands; a Native American woman might have been gathering firewood in a little clearing that is now the site of Rockefeller Center. What would she have thought if through some miracle she had straightened from picking up a fallen branch and found herself walking down the Fifth Avenue of today? She would see huge buildings, the world's greatest skyscrapers, automobiles and buses roaring along, and perhaps a plane or two soaring overhead. In the store windows she would see innumerable things that would mean absolutely nothing to her because she could not imagine a use for them. What could a food processor or a VCR or the thousand and one luxuries so beautifully displayed mean to her? They could mean nothing at all, because no one in her world had ever felt the need of them and so no one had ever conceived ideas of them. Where were all of these amazing things in the fifteenth century? They existed potentially in the realm of spiritual substance, which is the realm of Divine Mind. The substance of God-Mind, which is the spiritual substance of the universe, was always ready to pour itself into any idea that anyone might conceive and so project itself into form. The potentiality of everything our twentieth-century civilization can boast and everything that future civilizations can produce has always existed in God-Mind. It is the ever-ready supply that always meets the demand. God as our banker pays on demand—the demand of faith!

Jesus said, "According to your faith let it be done to you" (Mt. 9:29). Have faith in the omnipresence of God, for such faith enables you to say with assurance: *I cannot step out of God's abundant good.* Have faith in God's goodwill for you. This faith will enable you to affirm: *Because I am God's supreme creation, I cannot claim too much of God. My Father created me a channel of His own almightiness, an organ of His activity, and a vehicle of expression for Him.* Such faith is obeying prosperity's first commandment:

You shall look to no other source but God for your supply.

QUESTION HELPS

1. What is Truth?

2. What did Moses give to the Children of Israel in the form of the Ten Commandments?

3. What is the essential Truth of the first commandment? What relation does it have to permanent prosperity?

4. What are some of the promises of God regarding prosperity?

5. To what can we trace the poverty of the race? Of the individual?

6. What did Jesus mean by "stored-up" treasures?

7. Outline Jesus' instructions concerning prayer.

8. What limits our supply?

9. What relation do material avenues of supply bear to the source of supply?

10. What should be our attitude toward our
    debtors?

THE SECOND COMMANDMENT

You shall make no mental images of lack.

"You shall not make for yourself an idol, whether in the form of anything that is in heaven above, or that is on the earth beneath, or that is in the water under the earth. You shall not bow down to them or worship them; for I the Lord your God am a jealous God, punishing children for the iniquity of parents, to the third and the fourth generation of those who reject me, but showing steadfast love to the thousandth generation of those who love me and keep my commandments."

—Exodus 20:4-6

During their bondage in Egypt, the Israelites had absorbed many pagan superstitions and had, at times, faltered in their worship of the one God by seeking favor of the various Egyptian deities. When Moses returned from the mountain with the Ten Commandments, he found the people, weary of waiting for him, worshiping a golden calf that Aaron had made from their melted jewelry. We are told that Aaron "formed it in a mold, and cast an image of a calf" (Ex. 32:4).

We have long since outgrown idol worship, but

we have by no means outgrown the essential Truth in this commandment that we are not to create and serve false ideas. We still make "idols" and bow down to them, serve them, and fear them. These are the false beliefs that we are constantly engraving on our own minds and impressing on the minds of others through the power of suggestion. Every thought of poverty, fear, limitation, worry, and doubt is a false image, and every thought, word, and act of ours motivated by such thinking constitutes bowing down to "idols" and serving them. As a result, we have unfortunate conditions in life. The Lord our God is truly a "jealous God" in the sense of being an exacting God, and therefore His law of cause and effect takes severe toll of us. For every false belief we serve, we experience some unhappiness in life. Formulating and holding the belief is sowing the seed. The results that spring up in our lives are the unfortunate harvests that we have to reap.

When we substitute the word *exacting* for the word *jealous* and realize that the commandment refers to the inevitable action of God's laws in the mental realm, we better understand the rest of the commandment, which says that the sins or mistakes of parents are visited upon the children. Is it not true that our children and our children's children suffer through the false beliefs that we pass on to them? We fill the minds of these little ones who are delivered to our care with belief in the power of things to hurt them rather than with ideas of the power of God to help them. Take for example the two-year-old who, whenever she sneezed, was told by her elders, "You are catching cold." After a while she no longer waited to be told but, when she sneezed, would open her big eyes wide and run to the nearest grown-up crying, "Catching cold, catching cold!" Contrast this with an episode involving a small boy who had been brought up in Truth teaching. Seeing him on the street one rainy day, without boots, a neighbor said, "My dear, you'll take cold if you get your feet wet." The little fellow looked at her in surprise and, kicking a clump of grass at his feet, said, "It doesn't hurt the grass if its roots are wet, so why should it hurt me if my feet are wet?"

Rightly understood, the "iniquity of parents" is our heritage of mortal mind. The word *mortal* comes from the Latin word *mors*, meaning "death." Mortal mind is the total of all thoughts adverse to God and God's action, which is the all-knowing, all-loving action of eternal life. All thoughts that deny God's living presence are destructive of nature and therefore allied with death. Death and destruction exist only in mortal mind, which is the error consciousness of the human race, through which the mistaken beliefs of the whole human family continue to be imposed on generation after generation. Jesus showed us how to free ourselves from this error consciousness by accepting the truth of God's goodwill for us and holding steadfastly to it. He said, "You will know the truth, and the truth will make you free" (Jn. 8:32). We win our freedom from the "iniquity of parents"—our heritage of mortal mind—as we learn to use our divine heritage of spiritual understanding and let our thoughts dwell on God and boundless good. In so doing, we obey prosperity's second commandment:

You shall make no mental images of lack.

We hear a great deal about the creative power of thought. Correctly speaking, it is mind that is creative and thought is its action. Thought is the use we make of mind with its vast creative power. We often speak of a train of thought. It is a very good metaphor. A train is a vehicle that delivers something to a certain destination. So a train of thought is a vehicle of mind that delivers its creative power into manifestation. If we direct a train of thought to a mental image of lack, it will always arrive at its destination and unload creative power into this false image, and so we find ourselves building "Poverty Station." Every train of thought we direct toward it delivers its load of creative power, and Poverty Station fairly hums with activity. All the unhappy, sordid, fearsome beliefs of the thought realm gather there, and we find ourselves bowing down to them, serving them, and being held in such bondage by them that all other thought activity seems paralyzed. The way to demolish Poverty Station is to stop making mental images of lack and delivering trains of thought to them. Instead, we should practice using the creative power of mind to construct only the images of the good we desire to see made manifest.

Into the religion he gave the world, Jesus introduced the element of human mind action as the connecting link between the realm of Spirit and the world of form. This idea had been voiced in the Old Testament by the statement, "For as he thinketh in his heart, so is he" (Prov. 23:7 KJV). Jesus made this somewhat nebulous idea a positive teaching. He taught that like produces like. He said: "Are grapes gathered from thorns, or figs from thistles? In the same way, every good tree bears good fruit, but the bad tree bears bad fruit" (Mt. 7:16-17). Link this with, "The good person brings good things out of a good treasure, and the evil person brings evil things out of an evil treasure" (Mt. 12:35). What more clear-cut teaching could we have that the ideas which we hold in thought and feeling must eventually take form in our lives? With this teaching in mind, we understand why prosperity's second commandment is:

You shall make no mental images of lack.

We are constantly making mental images in connection with the thoughts we hold in mind. These
mental images are thought patterns that the
omnipresent energy of Divine Mind follows. All
the laws of the mental realm are called into operation until eventually the pattern is given concrete
form. If we have the thought of lack, we form
many mental images around it and see ourselves as
poor and in difficulty. We think and talk about it,
and in so doing, we bow down to this false image
and serve it; we pour our precious creative energy
into it and fix it ever more firmly in the realm of
form.

Since all appearances of lack have been brought
about by the wrong use of the creative energy of
mind, the remedy lies in making right use of this
same creative energy and so bringing the limitless
good of the invisible realm of Spirit into manifestation. It is easy to hold mental images of the things
that our senses register. It is difficult to repudiate
the evidence of the senses and persistently hold
mental images that conform to God's goodwill for
us. We know it is never God's will that we be
hungry, cold, destitute, or in want of any good
thing. Through spiritual substance, God has provided the wherewithal for the fulfilling of every
need, but we have to accept. Until we accept, there
is no consummation of God's gift to us of unlimited supply. It always takes two to make a gift. This

is illustrated in the parable of the prodigal son. The father quite definitely states that all he has belongs to his sons, yet one of them failed to benefit from his rich inheritance through his own willfulness in withdrawing from his father's house, and the son who stayed at home failed to benefit because he had placed himself in the position of a drudge and had never accepted his father's full bounty.

Like all of Jesus' parables, this one has a hidden meaning. Jesus often said in concluding a parable, "He who has ears to hear, let him hear" (Mt. 11:15 RSV), meaning that those who have some spiritual understanding can get more out of the lesson than appears on the surface. The deeper lesson of this parable is that we are all children of God, living in God's house of life. Some of us, like the prodigal, feel so self-sufficient that we take our divine heritage of life and intelligence and go out from the Father's house. We separate ourselves in thought and feeling from God as we make our home in that "far country"—the realm of mortal mind that is so far from the kingdom of God. We attach ourselves to some "citizen of that country," some lack and limitation that belongs to that state of mind, and eventually we find ourselves feeding "swine," that is, drudging for mere physical existence in most ignoble ways. The time comes when, like the prodigal in the story, we think of our Father and remember that it is His goodwill to give us all that we are willing to receive from Him. We remember that God needs only our confidence in His willingness and ability in order to rescue us from our mistakes and fulfill our good and just needs. That is when we, too, rise and go to our Father. We lift our thoughts from the present difficulty and thankfully acknowledge God's almighty power to make all things new. We stop making mental images of poverty and trouble and start imaging God's good for us. We may not see how it can be brought about, but we know God has offered us all that the heart can desire of His boundless good and we have only to accept in faith, believing we receive, in order to consummate the gift.

Many of us are like the other son in this parable, the one who stayed at home in the father's house. We love God and honestly try to serve Him, but our vision of His goodwill for us is very limited. Sometimes we, too, grow rebellious because we work so hard and try so hard and yet have so few of the good things our hearts crave. When the elder son in the parable was rebellious because the father had never showered him with gifts, his father's reply was, "Son, you are always with me, and all that is mine is yours" (Lk. 15:31). The son was a poor receiver, so engrossed with the idea of laboring for his father that he was blind to all that his father could and would do for him. All that his father had was his to use and enjoy, but his mind was so filled

with mental images of days of heavy labor with little or no reward that it never occurred to him to
ask and receive rich gifts that could bring him a
greater measure of happiness. He was bowing down
to a mental image of unrewarded labor and serving
it daily, even though he knew he was in his father's
house and wealth was all around him. In order to
receive his heart's desire, he had only to change
from his thought (mental image) of himself as a
servant, slaving away without reward to the true
thought of himself as his father's beloved son, asking and receiving his father's bounty.

Jesus always knew exactly what he wanted of his
heavenly Father. He knew his Father had already
fulfilled his every possible need in the realm of
Spirit, so that he had only to shape his desire
through the creative action of his own mind in
order to see it in manifestation. For instance, in all
matters of healing, he was keenly conscious of
God's presence as pure and perfect life. In each
case, his mind shaped the way he wished to see that
life manifest itself. His words revealed the image he
was holding of God's life. To the man with the
withered hand, he said, "Stretch out your hand"
(Mt. 12:13). He must have had a perfect image in
mind of a hand just as full of life activity as the rest
of the man's body. He could not possibly have told
him to stretch out his hand in full confidence of its
perfect normality if he had been holding on to the

mental image of a helpless, withered hand. When
he told blind men to open their eyes, he must have
had in his own mind a perfect image of God's life
expressing itself as healthy, normal eyesight. When
he fed the five thousand, he could not possibly have
been holding fast to a thought or mental image of
five loaves of bread and two small fishes. He must
have been seeing God's limitless substance manifesting as great quantities of bread and fish, enough
to feed thousands of hungry people. We know from
other miracles that he could control the elements of
nature through using his understanding of the laws
governing them. In the miracle of the loaves and
fishes, he must have controlled the creative activity
in the atom in order to produce instantaneous
increase. In all his miracles, he saw God's omnipresence manifesting itself in the form of his heart's
desire.

This shaping of the desire is the forming of the
mental image. The mental image is the mold that
the creative power of mind fills. Only when we
learn to obey prosperity's first commandment and
look to God for our supply are we able to hold
mental images of the fulfillment of our needs in the
face of all appearance to the contrary. When we
learn to do this, we are following Jesus' example.
We feel God's presence within us and all around us
as the perfect fulfillment of the need of the
moment. With joyous assurance, we can say: *With*

my mental tools, imagination, will, faith, and all my other glorious faculties, I fashion the mold that God fills. When we have asked God's guidance, and under His guidance shape our desires in this way, we are obeying prosperity's second commandment:

You shall make no mental images of lack.

QUESTION HELPS

1. What "idols" are we frequently making and serving today?

2. What do these images bring to us?

3. What do we mean by a "jealous God"?

4. What is the "iniquity of parents"? How is it visited on the children?

5. What is mortal mind? How may we free ourselves from its falsities?

6. What is the essential Truth of the second commandment? How may we apply it in establishing prosperity?

7. What did Jesus teach about the ideas we hold in mind?

8. How do we fashion the mold that God fills?

9. How is God's gift of limitless supply consummated?

10. What lessons may we learn from the parable of the prodigal son?

THE THIRD COMMANDMENT

You shall not speak the word of lack or limitation.

"You shall not make wrongful use of the name of the Lord your God, for the Lord will not acquit anyone who misuses his name."

—Exodus 20:7

It is a commonly accepted idea that the third commandment is a warning against blasphemy. While this is true, it is not generally understood that the blasphemous use of the name of the Deity involves much more than what is known as cursing.

Moffatt's translation of this passage into modern English reads as follows: "You shall not use the name of the Eternal, your God, profanely; for the Eternal will never acquit anyone who uses his name profanely."

Webster gives the following meaning of the word *profane:* "To debase by a wrong, unworthy, or vulgar use; to treat (something sacred) with abuse, irreverence, or contempt." All forms of cursing or swearing that contain a reference to the Deity come under this head. However, there are other ways in

which we are constantly using God's name profanely in our daily lives, and we suffer the inevitable
consequences of such wrong and unworthy use.

In order better to understand our constant violation of this third commandment, we must consider
the name of God that was delivered to Moses by
direct revelation. Spirit revealed itself to Moses as
pure Being. During Moses' experience of spiritual
exaltation, the voice of God resounded through his
consciousness, saying, "Thus you shall say to the
Israelites, 'I Am has sent me to you' " (Ex. 3:14). I
Am is the name of that living, loving, wise power,
which is pure being, the invisible reality of all that
is. I Am is also the name of our own indwelling
Spirit, the invisible image and likeness of God that
we are to make manifest as we fulfill the purpose of
our existence. Knowing this, we begin to understand that we are constantly creating difficulties in
our lives through making wrong use of the name of
God. When we say, "I am sick," "I am poor," we
are defiling God's name, and the fact that we do so
unintentionally makes little difference. Jesus said,
"On the day of judgment you will have to give an
account for every careless word you utter" (Mt.
12:36). Since the "day of judgment" is always the
period of reaping what we have sown in thought,
word, and action, we find that every destructive
claim we make in God's name is constantly taking
its toll of us.

The indiscriminate use of the I Am is not the only way of profaning God. Every destructive word is a libel against God, because it is a denial of God's presence. When we talk of poverty, we are affirming a falsehood, namely that there is an absence of the presence of God, All-Good. We can never become prosperous as long as we affirm poverty. Bearing this in mind, we find that in the third commandment the hidden Truth concerning prosperity is this:

You shall not speak the word of lack or limitation.

We hear a great deal about the power of the word. Mystically speaking, the word is the idea generated in mind. Commonly speaking, a word is a spoken or written symbol of an idea. From this point of view, we may say that the word gives form to the idea, for every spoken word launches some idea into the realm of form. It not only fixes the idea more firmly in our own minds but passes the idea on to other minds, causing them to form mental images that are in accord with the word spoken.

It has been said that we control our thoughts but our words control us. It is true that it is much easier to change a thought than it is to change the effect and the ensuing consequences of a spoken word. When we talk about our hard luck, our limited circumstances, the lack of any good thing in our lives, we reveal that we are making false images and letting them have power over us. We also reveal that we are not looking to God as the source of our supply. These first commandments are so closely interrelated that we cannot disobey one without disobeying all three.

The laws of mind go into operation through our words. Mind is threefold in nature—mind, idea, and expression. The word, whether oral, written, or expressed in actions, is always the expression of an idea in mind. Whenever an idea is expressed, whether it be true or false, the laws of mind work through it to an inevitable conclusion. If it is a false idea, the result will be a wrong answer to some problem of life. If it is a true idea, the result will be good—a right answer to one of life's problems. It is the expression of the idea, or word, that starts it on its way into the realm of form.

The apostle John saw in Jesus Christ the Word of God. He saw in him the living expression of ideas in Divine Mind. He said: "In the beginning was the Word, and the Word was with God, and the Word was God.... All things came into being through him, and without him not one thing came into being" (Jn. 1:1, 3). John saw that ideas of Divine Mind found expression through Jesus Christ. Being a spiritually illumined man, he understood that the word always expresses the idea generated in mind and starts it on its way into manifestation. He knew that every created thing comes into existence through the word, which is always the expression of an idea. He saw Jesus Christ as the personification of the word, that action of Divine Mind which gives form to ideas, the action through which the invisible is brought into visibility. Jesus Christ gave no expression to the false beliefs of mortal mind. His word was always a true word expressing a divine idea, and for that reason, it was always fulfilled.

Jesus told us, "By your words you will be justified, and by your words you will be condemned" (Mt. 12:37). When we have the idea of omnipresent Spirit as our unlimited source of supply, we are inspired to make mental images of the fulfillment of our needs according to God's goodwill, in spite of all appearances. Holding fast to these mental images, we speak only words of faith, hope, courage, and confident expectation of good, and by our words, we are justified.

On the other hand, every word of lack is the indication of a false mental image and is imbued with the creative power of mind through our persistent thought. As long as our words express these images, we are condemned to lack and limitation. Those of us who feel poor condemn ourselves to poverty through the persistency with which we talk about it, think about it, and allow our minds to be filled with poverty images.

It is difficult for us to realize that we need to

apply the same common sense in the realm of thought action as we do in the realm of outer action. If a cook makes a failure of a souffle, he or she does not just leave it alone to go running around expatiating on every detail of the catastrophe; instead he or she uses common sense and proceeds to remedy the mistake by doing the thing over in the right way. If executives make errors of judgment, they immediately proceed to rack their brains for ways and means of remedying them instead of telephoning all their business associates to call attention to their blunders.

If we make a mistake in working a mathematical problem, our common sense tells us that talking about it and calling other people's attention to it will not remedy it. The only remedy lies in going back to the principle involved, applying it, and so eradicating the mistake. If the mistake has been one of carelessness, we find it as we work the problem over according to principle. This same general idea applies to the realm of thought and feeling. If we are faced with a situation that fills us with fear and thoughts of lack, we need to use our common sense and set about remedying the situation, rather than talking about it. We need to revert to the principle involved—that there is an ever-present divine source of supply for every need—and let our thoughts and our words conform strictly to this principle.

The wise have learned that life is like an echo: it

always returns the call sent out. Like the echo, the response is always the same as the call, and the louder the call, the greater the response. When we talk of poverty, we get a poverty response in our circumstances. When we become frantic with fear and talk louder and longer about it, we only intensify the condition.

Truth students understand that life's echoing of our words is in accordance with the working of God's law, for our words are the culminating power of our thoughts, and our thoughts are the creative action of our minds. The spoken word is the first projection of the creative power of mind into the realm of form, and further manifestation always follows. The law is that whatever is persistently held in mind must eventually become manifest in the realm of form. We intensify the working of the law by every word we utter. When we think about a thing, we are forming a pattern of that particular thing; when we speak about it, we are sending forth the word and it is being condensed into form. We should not speak of an idea unless we want to see it take form. If we do not want it, we must wrestle with it in our minds until we succeed in eradicating it. We must loose the false idea and lay hold of a good one and, like Jacob wrestling with the angel, never let it go until it blesses us. When we accept it, we know that it has blessed us and then we can safely send it forth to be manifested through our spoken word.

The power of the word is recognized all through our Scriptures. In the Old Testament is the promise "You will decide on a matter, and it will be established for you" (Job. 22:28). Our word is always a decree. Its power depends on the forcefulness of the idea it expresses. When we say, "I am poor," we are decreeing poverty. The more emphatic we become, the more evidences of poverty we will see in our lives. Our word or decree is the expression of the mental image we are holding in mind. God's laws establish it—bring it into manifestation. Our part is decreeing or speaking the word; God's part is establishing in our lives the fulfillment of the word.

We cannot change the law, but we can always change the decree. The thing to remember is this: What we decree, God fulfills. This is a statement of partnership. Words of Truth deliver God's good into our lives when we speak them with conviction. When we know God as the source of our supply and express our faith in God by accepting only those ideas that we know are His goodwill for us, we speak words of courage, hope, and confident expectation of God's good; this is decreeing. The loving wisdom and power of the Almighty move through His immutable laws of the mental realm and fulfill our word in manifestation; this is the establishing of the decree.

Thought and word must be properly correlated

for right results. Jesus cautioned us against the use of "careless words," idle, empty words devoid of meaning. He assured us that even such words bring results eventually. Careless words express a careless, indifferent, or lazy state of mind and can only result in confusion in our affairs. Grand-sounding words are often empty and misleading. No words can be more meaningful than the ideas they convey. No matter how grandly we talk about our prospects and our accomplishments, if we know they are meager, our big talk will not improve them but will only add to the confusion in our affairs. Speaking the word of Truth does not mean talking big to the world. It means speaking words of quiet confidence in God's never-failing bounty. Such confidence only comes as a result of filling the mind with true ideas of God's goodwill and His limitless power to provide for every need. These ideas are generated through meditation, prayer, and affirmation.

Invoke the power of the word through both denial and affirmation. When confronted with an appearance of lack or limitation, deny that it has any place in God's plan for you; affirm your complete acceptance of God's bountiful provision for your every need. Work in prayer to gain the power of right thinking (remember Jacob and the angel) and then send that power forth through your spoken word to do the work whereunto it is sent. This is the way Jesus used the power of the word. In the

Old Testament, which was Jesus' Bible, is a statement that he knew was true for him: "So shall my word be that goes out from my mouth; it shall not return to me empty, but it shall accomplish that which I purpose, and succeed in the thing for which I sent it" (Is. 55:11).

Start watching your simplest words. Schiller said, "Only those who have the patience to do simple things perfectly will acquire the skill to do difficult things easily." Always remember that your words are forerunners of your circumstances. Be careful to speak only those words which you are willing to see take form in your life. Send forth your constructive word to create good and then stand fast in your faith in its creative power.

Affirm constantly: *I have faith in the power of my word. I speak only that which I desire to see made manifest.* Then decree steadfastly: *I am a living expression of God's abundant good. I receive and distribute God's never-failing bounty.* This is obeying prosperity's third commandment:

You shall not speak the word of lack or limitation.

QUESTION HELPS

1. What was the name of God revealed to Moses? How do we profane this holy name?

2. What is the essential Truth of the third commandment? In what way must we apply this truth if we would be prosperous?

3. Explain the threefold action of mind.

4. Why did John call Jesus "the Word" of God?

5. How do we condemn ourselves to poverty?

6. What is the commonsense way of correcting wrong thinking?

7. In what two ways do we invoke the power of the word?

8. What are "careless" words?

9. How do we increase the power of our word?

10. Explain "You will decide on a matter, and it will be established for you" (Job 22:28).

THE FOURTH COMMANDMENT

You shall let go and let God do it.

"Remember the sabbath day, and keep it holy. Six days you shall labor and do all your work. But the seventh day is a sabbath to the Lord your God; You shall not do any work—you, your son or your daughter, your male or female slave, your livestock, or the alien resident in your towns. For in six days the Lord made heaven and earth, the sea, and all that is in them, but rested the seventh day; therefore the Lord blessed the sabbath day and consecrated it."

—Exodus 20:8-11

In order to have a better understanding of the fourth commandment, we must know the true meaning of the word *Sabbath* and also the use the Hebrews made of numerical symbols in their ancient writings.

The word *Sabbath* means "a time of rest" (Webster). A Sabbath, then, is a period of cessation from effort in order to rest and relax for the purpose of gathering strength and power for a new period of activity. Moses instructed the Hebrews that such a period of perfect relaxation should be observed every seventh day because, to the Hebrew mind, the number seven was the symbol of rest and peace, the idea of completion or fulfillment following a period of activity. The number six symbolized satisfactory action in the relative realm. In the idea that God created the universe in six cycles of activity and rested during the seventh, we have the background of Moses' idea that not only human beings but all nature should do likewise.

In the natural world, the period of rest allows all forces of nature to gather strength for a new burst of activity. In the physical body, which is so closely allied to the natural realm, a period of rest enables the cells to store up reserve energy. In the mental realm, such a period of rest becomes a time of peace and quiet, enabling the mind to indulge in reflection on the things of the Spirit. This spiritual infilling is absolutely essential in all cycles of normal growth of the individual.

In every demonstration, there must be resting periods, times of cessation from outer activity, while one dwells in complete reliance on God and on the operation of His immutable laws.

It is evident, then, that the essential Truth in this commandment is that every period of well-rounded activity must be followed by a period of perfect peace and rest. In this understanding, we see that prosperity's fourth commandment may be worded thus:

You shall let go and let God do it.

We find many instances in the New Testament showing us how Jesus conformed to the idea in this commandment in making his great demonstrations. He would go apart to pray, and after such a period of infilling, he would move through a period of intense activity of teaching and healing; then he would go apart to rest awhile. His resting period would in turn be followed by another cycle of work. In these periods of activity, we have many instances of Jesus' acknowledging his heavenly Father in prayer before performing some miracle of healing that we would call a demonstration. From Jesus, we get the perfect model of the way to make a demonstration: pray, work, rest, then repeat the cycle.

Our major difficulty in making any demonstration lies in the fact that the personal self, the willful Adam, insists on assuming the entire responsibility and so prevents us from receiving the beneficence of the divine will. We need to learn that our part lies in acknowledging God's presence, accepting from God the good we desire, doing whatever is logically required of us to further this desire, and then letting God do His part through His already established laws.

Again let us follow Jesus' example and look to nature for an illustration. The farmer selects the seed; this may be likened to the exercise of volition in deciding what we want. Next he prepares the

ground before planting the seed; this is like the
period of prayer in which we acknowledge the one
Source from which can come the harvest or fulfillment of the desire. The third step is the planting of
the seed; this may be likened to the act of accepting
from God the particular thing desired, the planting
in the soil of mind the idea that is to be made
manifest. There is still another step to be taken on
the farmer's part: he must tend the seed by keeping
it well watered and free from weeds. We tend the
seed idea planted in mind by pouring out our faith
upon it and uprooting, through the use of denial
and affirmation, all thoughts of fear, doubt, and
worry.

After having done his part, the farmer can only
wait with confidence for the harvest. He cannot
send the first root down into the ground, nor can
he create that first upward shoot of green. He cannot put the leaf and the flower on the stalk, and he
cannot transform the flower into the fruit. This is
God's part, God working through the natural laws
that He has established, according to His own
divine will. He follows through and does His part
in cooperation with the farmer. How small the
farmer's part, and how great God's part! Yet the one
is contingent on the other.

Just as the farmer, having done his part, has to
wait on God's action through natural law, so we,
having done our part in the mental realm, have to

learn to let go and let God do His part through the action of spiritual laws.

Often we are unable to sleep because we cannot rest from our problems. We keep on trying to solve them by thinking about them long after the day's work is over. We haven't sufficient faith in God to place ourselves and all our affairs in His safekeeping while mind and body rest quietly, gathering strength and energy for further activity. Because Jesus had such perfect trust in his heavenly Father, he could loose and let go the problems of the day. He could place himself and all his affairs in God's care and rest serenely and peacefully no matter what the forces that stormed around him. In the story of the storm on the Sea of Galilee, we have a wonderful example of his ability to rest in perfect trust in God. He and the Apostles had come to the end of a day of teaching, healing, and ministering to the needs of many people. The time had come for a well-earned period of rest. They embarked in a small boat and set sail upon the sea at eventide. Jesus fell asleep immediately. The elements were stormy and the Apostles were fearful, and so they remained awake. They became more terrified as the storm increased, and in their fright awakened Jesus. They were crying, "Teacher, do you not care that we are perishing?" (Mk. 4:38) In telling the story afterward, they said that he rebuked the wind and the waves, and all became calm once more. He also rebuked the Apostles, saying, "Have you still no faith?" (Mk. 4:40) It was evident that their faith was in the power of wind and wave to harm them rather than in the power of God to protect and care for them. They had done God's work during the day, but they were unable to trust Him to work for them while they rested.

The feeling of partnership with God is essential in all successful living. First we need to feel that God can be relied on to guide our thoughts and words and actions; then we must realize that the same power that inspires us to do the right thing is the power that provides us with the necessary strength and ability to follow through. But the partnership does not end here. After we have done everything we know how to do, we can safely rest from our labors, knowing that God carries on and that when there is more work for us to do, it will be revealed to us. It has been said that God works in mysterious ways to perform His wonders. When through our own gallant efforts we have rid our minds of doubts and fears and are truly trusting in Him, we find that a seemingly chance word or contact is the next step in the demonstration of the good we desire. These things amaze us until we remember that while we have been resting, God has continued working through His immutable laws of mind and, as a result, has drawn into our lives whatever we need as surely as a magnet draws iron filings.

Loosing the problem and letting God solve it does not mean that we are entirely released from all responsibility concerning our affairs. Jesus' illustration of the lilies of the field—"They neither toil nor spin, yet I tell you, even Solomon in all his glory was not clothed like one of these" (Mt. 6:28-29)—has been much misunderstood. The lazy type of mind, the mind that is always looking for a chance to shirk responsibility, interprets it as meaning that one only needs to pray and then do nothing whatever toward helping oneself. As a matter of fact, the lilies of the field are constantly busy at the business of growing and producing blossom and seed. They are automatically obedient to the natural laws under which they function. Every lily is being true to its own inherent nature and doing exactly what is expected of the lily idea of Divine Mind. Jesus was pointing out that the lily grows without struggle or effort, just letting God's laws furnish all that it needs to use in its business of growing. When we can learn to be true to our own inherent nature and do only those things that we are intended to do, we, too, will find that our needs are beautifully met without struggle and competition.

Speaking of the person whose life is established in well-being, an Indian mystic once said, "He attains his end because he does not interfere with the higher power." We need to learn noninterference. Having done our part, we must "Be still before the Lord, and wait patiently for him" (Ps. 37:7). This waiting patiently does not mean being inactive. It means living in a quiet state of confident expectation that all which is necessary to complete our demonstration is being done in the realm of divine ideas and projected into form through the medium of mental laws, while we move serenely on our way, constructive, creative units in God's world. One of the surest evidences of faith in God is our being able to turn away from a difficult situation in which we have done our best, to give our attention to other matters with calm, untroubled minds.

When we do not at once see the result desired and can think of no new effort to make, we are prone to be discouraged. It is at such a time that we need to pour out our faith, pluck out the ideas of discouragement and doubt, and know that *it is being done.* That which is completed at the moment when you accept in faith, believing, is on its way to manifestation through the medium of mental laws. Remember that these laws work not only in your mind but in the minds of all God's children. Every person who touches your life is a potential instrument of God's action in manifesting your good. You never know what contacts are being made, what action is going on in this invisible realm of mind. But remember this: If you are doing your part, you can safely take a rest from even thinking about your demonstration. You can joyously know that the work of manifestation goes on as you rest from effort and let the joy of the Lord fill you as you relax.

A good formula for demonstration is as follows: First, have faith in Omnipresence, declaring: *You created me and You sustain me, dear Father-Mother God, and You can handle my affairs.* Second, have faith in God's goodwill for you. Affirm: *I accept of You now, O blessed Spirit, this desired good. I am alert and receptive to all that You would have me do in bringing this to pass.* Third, think, speak, and act in accordance with your desire, and do whatever you feel you are guided to do in the realm of outer action to bring it to pass. Last—and of the utmost importance—having done your part, keep your mind busy with something else that is constructive, creative, or recreational in nature. Rest from the idea of the demonstration you wish to make, knowing that the Spirit dwelling in you knows the Father's way and always does what it sees the Father do.

"Return, O my soul, to your rest, for the Lord has dealt bountifully with you" (Ps. 116:7). This mode of demonstration is in obedience to prosperity's fourth commandment:

You shall let go and let God do it.

QUESTION HELPS

1. Explain the meaning of the word *Sabbath*.

2. What is the symbolical significance of the number seven?

3. What happens during rest periods in the natural world? In the physical body? In the mental realm?

4. What is the essential Truth of the fourth commandment? How can we apply it in demonstrating prosperity?

5. Describe the model for demonstration that Jesus set for us.

6. Give an illustration of the way nature follows this perfect model.

7. What is meant by noninterference?

8. What is the lesson of the "lilies of the field"?

9. What is the surest evidence of faith in God?

10. Give a good formula for demonstration.

THE FIFTH COMMANDMENT

You shall deal honorably with God and with all human instruments through whom God's good is manifested for you.

"Honor your father and your mother, so that your days may be long in the land that the Lord your God is giving you."

—Exodus 20:12

When Moses delivered the Ten Commandments to the Children of Israel, he furnished an unruly people with a moral basis of right action toward God and humanity. The first four commandments have to do with right action toward God, and the last six with right action toward humanity. Each ethical or moral instruction is but a garment of Truth, for Truth itself is the basic principle of all right action.

On the surface, the fifth commandment exhorts us to act ethically toward our earthly parents. All ethical action is based on justice, honesty, and cooperation. We are told to honor our father and mother, to be just and honest in our dealing with them, and to cooperate with them in all ways. The word *honor* carries within its meaning all this and more, for it also implies courtesy and the rendering of due obedience. There is still another meaning in the word *honor*: to honor a draft is "to live up to or fulfill the terms of," according to Webster. In truly honoring our parents, we make application of all these meanings, even the one "to live up to or fulfill the terms of." We accepted our physical bodies from them, and we accepted their care during infancy, childhood, and adolescence. When we obey the fifth commandment, we accept an obligation and gladly pay it when it falls due. In other words, when our parents in turn need our loving care and we are able to use in their service the bodies they nurtured and the minds they disciplined and instructed, we are under obligation to do so.

The fifth commandment begins the instruction concerning right action toward our fellow human beings. Logically, it starts with right action toward our parents. We may think of life as a series of concentric circles, and only as we learn to act wisely and well within the smallest circle, the immediate family, do we develop the ability to establish standards of right action to guide us in relation to the ever-extending circles of friends, business associates, and local, national, and world groups.

Spiritually awakened people see their earthly fathers and mothers as the human instruments through which God's law has worked to provide them with a physical body to serve God as they go about the business of living God's life for Him here on earth. Spiritually awakened people know themselves as spiritual beings and God as their progenitor. They know this same truth for their fathers and mothers. They honor their parents for their part in enabling the awakened people to continue working out their mission, the manifesting of the spirit God has given them. Thomas Aquinas, the great Italian theologian of the thirteenth century, makes it very plain that if we are unable to be grateful for the physical life bestowed by our parents, we are unable to be grateful for the spiritual life that God bestowed on us. In *The Commandments of God*, he says: "Natural life is nothing as compared with the life of grace. If then you fail to acknowledge the blessing of the natural life which you owe to your parents, you are unworthy of the life of grace which is greater, and still more unworthy of the life of glory which is the greatest of all the blessings." The life of grace is our Father's free gift to us of His own spiritual life, and the life of glory can only be the splendor of that life when made manifest, as in Jesus Christ.

With the eye of inner vision, we look through our earthly parentage to our divine progenitor, our heavenly Father. We honor Him not only as the source of life but the source of all supply, and we see exhortation to deal honorably with Him in prosperity's fifth commandment:

You shall deal honorably with God and with all human instruments through which God's good is manifested for you.

We are to be courteous and render due obedience to God as the giver of all good gifts, and since we are constantly accepting His bounty, we are in justice bound to give Him what is His due.

The law of compensation teaches us to return full value always. All the laws of life operate in accord toward the end of establishing perfect balance on all planes of our existence. If we do not consciously endeavor to give full value always for what we receive, the subconscious action of our minds always moves toward establishing balance at some time, in some way. The sooner we learn to discharge our just obligation as we progress daily, the sooner we will find ourselves established in more harmonious, better-balanced ways of living.

We gladly accept from God, but we are prone to forget that there is something justly due to Him from us. When making a demonstration, we are accepting God's law working in our behalf; when the demonstration is completed, we must pay what is justly due God if we would deal honorably with Him. One of the necessary ways of establishing ethical conduct toward God is the practice of tithing. The tither is obeying the injunction:

"Honor the Lord with your substance and with the first fruits of all your produce" (Prov. 3:9).

To honor the Lord with our substance is to render inner service to acknowledge His presence in prayer, praise, and silent worship. To honor Him with the first fruits of our produce is to render outer service, to give a just portion of the supply we demonstrate to the maintenance of His work here on earth.

Rightly understood, tithing is a form of worship. True prayer must include acknowledgment. There is no surer way of acknowledging God as the source of supply than the actual giving back to God a portion of all that we have received from God. We may acknowledge God as our source of supply in silence and in words and still not actually show our faith before we put this acknowledgment into action. The only way to go into action on any belief is to express it in tangible form. Tithing is really the outer aspect of the threefold nature of worship: prayer, praise, giving. To be prayerful, praiseful, and bountiful in giving is to worship truly.

Viewed from a practical angle, tithing is accounting to God for what we receive. It is actual recognition of God as the source of supply; without tithing, the recognition is purely theoretical. We may say, then, that tithing is a guarantee of our good faith in God as our supply. It is recognition of God's ownership and our stewardship. Tithing indicates an understanding of the working of the law of increase in human affairs. We see this law working in nature: every harvest is an increase or multiplication of the seeds originally planted. Some part of the harvest must be given back to nature if there is to be a future harvest. The same law is operative in the realm of human affairs. A just portion of all that is received from God must be given back to God to support His work.

The question often arises, "Why do we give a tenth of all that we demonstrate rather than some other portion?" The answer is that the mystics of all ages, particularly those of the Hebrew race, assigned certain symbolic values to numbers, and the number ten is always the number of increase. Mathematically speaking, with each count of ten we begin a new series of numbers, entering a new cycle of increase. Since the number ten, then, symbolizes increase, it is logical to use a tenth of the wealth we demonstrate as our "prosperity seed," which we return to the source from which it came, knowing that as it is put to work it produces ever increasingly rich harvests of God's bounty in our lives. The idea of increase as associated with tithing works both ways: it increases our service to God and increases God's supply in our lives.

Jesus mentioned tithing on only two occasions, once in a parable and once when addressing a group of Pharisees. Each time he spoke of it in a way that indicated that he considered it a matter to be taken for granted. "Woe to you, scribes and Pharisees, hypocrites! For you tithe mint, dill, and cummin, and have neglected the weightier matters of the law: justice and mercy and faith. It is these you ought to have practiced without neglecting the others" (Mt. 23:23). It was Paul's teaching that "the letter kills, but the Spirit gives life" (2 Cor. 3:6), so tithing as a mere outer action performed with the idea of gaining favor with God is of no value in the life of the individual. Jesus made this plain when he said again to the Pharisees: "You tithe mint and rue and herbs of all kinds, and neglect justice and the love of God; it is these you ought to have practiced, without neglecting the others" (Lk. 11:42). It is evident that Jesus was rebuking the Pharisees because they were worshiping God according to the letter of the law of Moses, but the true spirit of worship was not in their hearts. To be efficacious, tithing, like prayer, must be a matter of inner feeling as well as outer action. The outer form is like an empty shell. It is the feeling that accompanies it that makes both tithing and prayer of inestimable value in our lives.

All religious work should be supported by the tithes of those who receive its blessings. At the time of Jesus' earthly ministry, the Temple in Jerusalem and all other temples of worship were entirely supported by the tithes, the first fruits of the increase from cattle, farm produce, and business investments. The early Christian churches were supported in the same way. Paul sent these instructions to one group: "On the first day of every week, each of you is to put aside and save whatever extra you earn, so that collections need not be taken when I come" (1 Cor. 16:2). Where there is conscientious tithing to a religious cause, no special collections are ever necessary. Raising money in other ways for the maintenance of religious work is proof that those who support it have not yet learned to "Honor the Lord with your substance and with the first fruits of all your produce" (Prov. 3:9).

Jesus himself gave all to God. Giving all frees us from tithing, just as obeying Jesus' new commandment frees us from all Mosaic law. We shall never learn to follow after him in the new dispensation (which is the life of Spirit lived under the law of grace) and truly give all until we learn to give systematically that portion which is considered just under the old dispensation (the life of the intellect lived under the Mosaic law).

Since Truth students know God as the source of supply and also understand the law of giving and receiving, why do so many still withhold the tithe? For two reasons: selfishness (which is greed) and fear. In the first instance, the acquisitive instinct is still so strong that it blinds them to the realization that they are not only receivers but disbursers of

God's bounty. They may accumulate riches through their deep-seated faith that God's limitless supply is theirs to draw on, but in time they will learn that just as the manna in the wilderness became putrid when hoarded, so wealth selfishly held eventually brings trouble in its wake. Those who are not of the selfish or acquisitive type withhold the tithe through fear. They think they have faith in God as the source of their supply, but they are really deceiving themselves in so thinking, for they are afraid to let go of what they have for fear they may later on lack some good thing they desire. Their actions prove that they place far more trust in material things than in God. For instance, they would not think of depending on just the water in the pipes in their bathroom for a bath. They would cheerfully use that water to clean the tub, knowing that there is unlimited supply behind, pushing its way forward, ready to be used. When they learn to think of God as a reservoir from which a continuous stream of abundance flows into their lives, they will no longer place their dependence on the money in their pocketbooks or bank accounts. They will depend only on the limitless source of all supply, knowing that as they use what they now have cheerfully and wisely, the flow from the source will be continuous.

Faith in God always counteracts fear. As we give more of ourselves in meditation, prayer, and service, we grow steadily in the realization of God's presence in all and through all; we become increasingly aware of His power moving through His Spirit dwelling in us to fulfill our needs on all planes of existence. As we increase our faith in God as the ever-present beneficence, we learn to take what has been called "the first adventurous step in walking with God" and give a tenth of our increase to His service. God is our Father and Mother, the divine Progenitor, who conceived and gestated the idea of us in Divine Mind and expressed or gave birth to that idea when creating us in His own image. Honor God that you may continue to enjoy bounty, "so that you may long remain in the land that the Lord your God is giving you for all time" (Deut. 4:40). As you let justice, honesty, and cooperation govern your action toward God and all human instruments through whom you receive His benefits, you are obeying prosperity's fifth commandment:

You shall deal honorably with God and with all human instruments through whom God's good is manifested for you.

QUESTION HELPS

1. With what do the first four commandments deal? The last six?

2. On what is all ethical action based?

3. Define the word *honor.*

4. What is our true relationship to our earthly parents? To God?

5. How may we honor our earthly parents? How may we honor God?

6. What is the essential Truth of the fifth commandment? How may we apply it in establishing permanent prosperity?

7. Explain "Honor the Lord with your substance and with the first fruits of all your produce" (Prov. 3:9).

8. What is tithing? Why is one-tenth considered a suitable tithe?

9. Why do some Truth students withhold the tithe?

10. How are faith and tithing related?

THE SIXTH COMMANDMENT

You shall not take your wealth out of circulation.

"You shall not kill."
—Exodus 20:13 RSV

Every commandment that is of God voices an essential Truth. This Truth is applicable in the life of every member of the human race at all stages of existence. In the sixth commandment, "You shall not kill," we again have such an essential Truth. It is a grave mistake to limit the meaning of this commandment to the taking of human life. So construed, it ceases to be of further value to those who have evolved to the point where the idea of taking human life is abhorrent. Since a commandment of God never ceases to be an essential Truth, to be obeyed constantly by everyone, we must look to the idea incorporated in the word *kill* for enlightenment. To kill is to destroy. A slanderous word can kill a reputation. Many a peaceful home situation has been broken up through destructive words, words that kill confidence and destroy happiness. We often kill our own ideals through destructive thoughts of fear or doubt, or through letting influences of our own lower nature gain ascendancy.

All that is evil is allied with death and destruction. Evil thoughts and words are killers, and those who exercise them are disobeying the sixth commandment.

There is a still more subtle idea connected with the word *kill*. Again, the idea of death is incorporated in it. Death is disintegration. Stagnation is the starting point of all disintegration, and lack of circulation is the cause of stagnation. We find, then, in this commandment an exhortation to keep our good in circulation. As we circulate the gifts of God, they increase in our lives in proportion to their increase of value in the lives of others. For instance, if we desire more love in our lives, we must lay hold of our spiritual love nature, establish love in our hearts, and give it out freely. Words of kindness, thoughtfulness, and friendliness are carriers of love to the minds that receive them. In all hearts, even the heart of the most hardened person, there is a wellspring of love; for love, wisdom, and power are inherent in life itself. We often hear the expression, "Her heart was touched." What this really means is that the love nature of her being responded compassionately to a call of need, or happily to a call of kindliness. The same kindly word that opens up the love nature of the individual carries her love back to the speaker of the word.

It may be shown in a hundred different ways.

It is a great Truth that "love begets love." We have only to start practicing the circulation of loving thoughts, words, and actions to prove this. It is correspondingly true that if we desire much joy and happiness, we must radiate more happiness into the lives of others. If we want more vigor and vitality, we must put to work the physical energy we already have. If we want success and prosperity, we must use to the utmost what is already ours. In other words, stagnation is death, but circulation is life. Prosperity's sixth commandment, therefore is this:

You shall not take your wealth out of circulation.

These few words voice one of the greatest lessons that we have to learn concerning permanent prosperity. Just as we cannot have healthy bodies without good circulation, so we cannot have healthy circumstances unless our wealth circulates freely.

Jesus gave a powerful illustration of this Truth in his parable of the talents. There are a number of lessons in this particular parable. The first is that God's is the ownership and ours the stewardship. The second is found in the words "to each according to his ability" (Mt. 25:15). The idea is that we are expected to make good use of what we have demonstrated at any given point in our development; that is, keep it in circulation. We all have our own particular abilities; we have developed our

God-power in different ways and to different degrees. Each person is expected to use his or her present abilities in such a way as to increase them and in so doing develop greater abilities or gifts.

It is evident that Jesus intended this teaching to be applied not only to the developing of our spiritual gifts, but also to the handling of our material wealth. If it were not so, he would not have used money transactions as an illustration. The two servants who used their Lord's money wisely by putting it into circulation and increasing it were highly praised and generously rewarded. The one who was afraid and, through hoarding it, took the money out of circulation could show no increase of the riches that had been entrusted to his care. We are told that he was not only severely reprimanded but that even the little he had was taken away from him. The implications of this parable may be expanded to yield a great number of teachings of deep spiritual value. One of these teachings has to do with prosperity. It reveals that circulation is the secret of increase. If we are to prosper, there must be circulation not only of rich ideas in mind but also of the wealth that is the manifestation of these ideas.

Fear and condemnation are allied with stagnation and death. Fear kills faith and prevents the divine ideas of God's almighty power and infinite goodwill from circulating freely in mind and affairs.

Condemnation kills praise and appreciation. When we criticize and condemn our circumstances, we have no appreciation of God's presence with us as our unfailing source of all good. There can be no circulation of God's good where there is no praise of God's presence. When the pocketbook is empty and the bank account limited, there should be no condemnation of either. They should be blessed with divine persistency. Webster's dictionary says that *to bless* is to "praise, glorify; endow, favor; to confer prosperity or happiness upon." You glorify your pocketbook or bank account when you praise or give thanks for the everywhere-present spiritual substance that you know fills it to overflowing and takes the form of the funds desired according to your faith. Instead of condemning, you are granting "divine favor" to these receptacles of your divine abundance as you behold them filled to overflowing with the material evidence of God's goodwill for you. By blessing instead of condemning, you truly "confer prosperity upon" your circumstances.

Praise and faith are allied with circulation and life. Through praise and faith, we keep our consciousness alive to God's presence and so keep God's good circulating in our lives. Wealth that is the result of faith in God's never-failing bounty and infinite goodwill can never hurt or harm. The possessors of such wealth love the source from which it comes, God, and not the wealth itself. They do not depend on possessions for happiness; they know that happiness rests with God. Though circumstances may sweep away all possessions, they need not be unhappy because it is God's good pleasure to pour fresh riches into their lives.

Those who depend on worldly possessions for happiness will always be restless souls. It says in our Scriptures, "The lover of money will not be satisfied with money" (Eccles. 5:10). Those who give love to material things can never be satisfied; the more they have, the more they want, and the more unscrupulous they may become in trying to satisfy their craving. Material things—money and all that it can buy—are not evil in themselves. It is the love of these things that develops greed and selfishness and kindred evils in people's minds. We read in the New Testament: "For the love of money is a root of all kinds of evil, and in their eagerness to be rich some have wandered away from the faith and pierced themselves with many pains" (1 Tim. 6:10).

There is an interesting story in Greek mythology that illustrates graphically the sorrow that love of money can bring. We often speak figuratively of a person who has accumulated much wealth as having the "Midas touch," meaning that everything that person touches seems to turn to gold. The idea of the Midas touch is based on an ancient myth concerning the god Dionysus and Midas, the king of Phrygia. In return for a favor, Dionysus granted

Midas one wish. Midas had the ambition to be the richest man in the world, so he greedily wished that all that he touched would turn to gold. For a while he enjoyed the thrill of seeing his throne and all the furnishings of his palace turn to gold at his slightest touch. He then wandered into the garden and plucked one of its rare blooms, thinking to enjoy its fragrance. But, alas, it turned to gold in his hand. He returned to the palace in a thoughtful mood and, being hungry, ordered food. But the food turned to gold, and he sat troubled and hungry at a table laden with rich viands. Just then his little daughter, whom he loved more dearly than anyone else in the world, came into the room and ran into his outstretched arms—and turned into a little golden statue! In deepest despair, he prayed earnestly to his god, begging release from the curse that had once been his heart's desire. Dionysus sent him to wash in a certain river. He hastened to obey the command. He dipped himself in the river and came out with asses' ears, but free from the curse of gold. The implication is that he who sets gold above all else is a fool!

When money is relegated to its rightful place in life, it becomes an outer symbol of God's abundance, a recognized medium of exchange of value for value received. When money is wisely used as a medium of exchange, it embodies equity and honor. Our Scriptures link money and wisdom, indicating that the two must be inseparable when money is rightly understood and rightly used. It says in Ecclesiastes: "The protection of wisdom is like the protection of money" (Eccles. 7:12). Money is an outer symbol of God's defense against lack and limitation. Like all good, it must be kept in circulation.

It has been said that "richness should circulate through our affairs as air does through our lungs." We know that there is no good circulation of air in the lungs unless the exhalations balance the inhalations. When air does not circulate freely through the lungs, the result is congestion, which results in diseased conditions and may eventually cause death. Again, we have an illustration of the fact that stagnation is death and circulation is life.

In our present civilization, money is the life stream of the economic realm. It must be kept in circulation in order to do its work. Any economic system is a man-made plan of distribution of supply and has a spiritual counterpart that is the result of an unconscious spiritual urge to establish law and order and balance in the matter of supply. As long as money circulates freely, an economic system flourishes. When money ceases to circulate, disintegration sets in and the system slowly dies, until through some stimulus, money starts circulating again and so resuscitates it.

We see the economics of God working throughout the realm of nature. Plant life absorbs freely all that nature offers of light, heat, and nourishment. It uses creatively all that is received and then gives back its creation to the soil. It gives back the seed that it may grow and increase, and it also gives back leaf, stem, and stalk to enrich the soil for the nourishing of the new seed. Nothing is wasted. There is a continuous action of receiving and giving in an endless cycle.

There is a saying, "As the macrocosm so the microcosm"—as the great so the small. Each individual is a miniature universe. The laws that we see operative in the universe around us are also operative in our own minds, bodies, and circumstances. We have within ourselves God-given potentialities that may be likened to the raw material that under divine guidance we can mold into our outer needs. Through faith in the spiritual power and substance within ourselves and in the universe around us, we can demonstrate supply. However, knowledge of the economics of God, the laws under which God's good functions, is necessary to keep the supply constantly in evidence. The economics of God are very simple: We receive justly for all that we give, and we must give freely if we would receive freely. We must keep our good in circulation not only in thought and word but in the realm of action, where the use we make of our money is always revealed. There are many ways of keeping money wisely circulated. Two of the most important ways are giving to God and to other people. Using money for only selfish purposes is a form of hoarding. It is confining the use of money to the purposes of an individual. While this keeps the money itself in circulation, there is a state of congestion in the mind of the individual who is self-centered in using money, and this person eventually finds that money is not bringing comfort in mind or in circumstances.

Riches are a state of mind. The person who has money and uses it intelligently—keeping it in circulation unselfishly and getting enjoyment out of it—is rich. The one who has it and hoards it, or the one who uses it only for selfish purposes, is still poor, no matter how much that person has. The miser, for instance, is not rich, but merely a collector—collecting stocks, bonds, other securities, and cash, and leading a harried, worried existence, constantly obsessed with the fear of loss of possessions. Most miserly traits can be traced to fear of poverty. All fear is congestion in the realm of mind, bred of a sense of separation from the divine source of supply. The person who has faith in God as the never-failing resource uses money fearlessly and joyously, knowing that free and intelligent use of it is a guarantee of its increase. Such a person understands and obeys the sixth commandment:

You shall not take your wealth out of circulation.

QUESTION HELPS

1. What other thoughts are incorporated in the word *kill* besides the actual taking of life?

2. What is the relation between stagnation and death? Between circulation and life?

3. What is the essential Truth of the sixth commandment? How does it apply to our prosperity?

4. What is the first lesson of the parable of the talents? Explain the second lesson in the parable.

5. What is the secret of increase?

6. What thoughts must we keep circulating if we would have more happiness? More health? More wealth?

7. In what way are fear and condemnation "killers"?

8. In what way are praise and faith related to
    circulation and life?

9. Explain the economics of God.

10. What does money wisely used symbolize?

THE SEVENTH
COMMANDMENT

You shall not abase your wealth to idle or evil uses.

"You shall not commit adultery"
—Exodus 20:14

The seventh commandment has to do with purity. In teaching the necessity of purity, Moses had to meet his people on their own level of consciousness. They were a people at a stage in their development when they were more capable of understanding rules of right action applicable to their daily lives than spiritual truths that have to do with soul development. So Moses impressed on them the necessity of cleaving to the chosen mate in love and loyalty when he delivered the law: "You shall not commit adultery."

Like all essential Truth, the ideal of purity must be served in outer as well as inner action. To use the life force promiscuously for the sole purpose of gratifying the sensual nature is to debase a spiritual power by using it unworthily, and under the law of cause and effect, all unworthy use of spiritual power brings dire results. We find this idea in the admonition: "Do you not know that you are God's temple and that God's Spirit dwells in you? If anyone destroys God's temple, God will destroy that person. For God's temple is holy, and you are that temple" (1 Cor. 3:16-17). We know that every destructive thought defiles the temple and does its part in destroying or tearing it down. Such thoughts often bring about the sensual use of the life forces. Without the purifying element of a higher form of love, such sensual use defiles the body and is one of the greatest factors in the race consciousness tending to destroy it.

The word *adultery* comes from the same root as the word *adulterate*, which, according to Webster, means "to corrupt, debase, or make impure by the addition of a foreign or inferior substance." We have heard a great deal about adulterating foods with harmful or less nourishing ingredients. Because of this similarity in meaning, we may then define the word *adultery*, in its deeper sense, as the act of making impure, or of weakening or rendering harmful, by mixing with something of a base or foreign nature. This applies not only to physical but to mental action.

Jesus taught that defiling the mind with impure thoughts was as great an evil as debasing the body by sensual uses. He drove home the lesson that all impure action is but the manifestation of impure thought. It is evident, then, that the seventh commandment is not to be interpreted as dealing only with one type of impurity. We find incorporated in the seventh commandment an essential Truth that applies to all thought action. This commandment is closely allied with the first three commandments, which have to do with the necessity of keeping the eye single. In the seventh commandment, we are exhorted to maintain purity of thought and action. We are not to debase our spiritual ideals by yielding to the temptations of our sense appetites. This idea is to be applied not only in establishing health and happiness but also in establishing prosperity. Our supply is of God; it is an outer symbol of omnipresent good. If it is to be a lasting blessing, with happiness in its wake, it must be handled in a way becoming to the nature of the source whence it comes. With this idea in mind, it becomes clear to us that prosperity's seventh commandment can be stated in the following terms:

You shall not abase your wealth to idle or evil uses.

Money is an outer form of spiritual substance. Like all form, it has only the life and power of the divine idea that animates it. The animating idea in money is supply. Money is a medium of exchange used in modern civilization for the supplying of material needs. When we awaken to the Truth that God is the source of supply, we recognize money as a symbol of God's abundance.

Realizing this, we see our responsibility to use

money intelligently. Just as the body temple is destroyed by destructive thoughts that defile it, so our financial security, which is a part of our circumstances or our "extended body," suffers through our evil use of it.

The creative process in mind through which prosperity is demonstrated is clearly indicated in the first three of prosperity's ten commandments:

You shall look to no other source but God for your supply.

You shall make no mental images of lack.

You shall not speak the word of lack or limitation.

We look to God—omnipresent spiritual substance or divine energy—as the one Source from which our good can come. We know that divine energy quickens our thoughts (mental images) and words, and fills them with the creative power that projects them into the world of form. When we associate our wealth with thoughts of greed, selfishness, or lust, we defile our minds and make base use of God's golden stream of spiritual substance, which carries within itself the potential of limitless supply for every need. When we associate unworthy thoughts with wealth, we make unworthy use of wealth. When we make unworthy use of God's good, the laws of life take bitter toll of us, and we pay in terms of disaster. When we make worthy use of God's good, we have the joy of seeing it increase in our lives, and we have obeyed the biblical exhortation, "But remember the Lord your God, for it is he who gives you power to get wealth" (Deut. 8:18).

There are many ways of making evil use of money. The most common is to use it to pamper worldly appetites. Every such use takes severe toll of the individual, frequently resulting in loss of the money itself. People whose minds are made sluggish through overindulgence of appetites may lose the fortune that makes such indulgence possible. Even though the money itself is not lost, the individual often loses the ability to enjoy it.

Often wealth is used to gratify lust for power. People become "money mad" and use their wealth ruthlessly in order to increase it and to satisfy their ambition. Dishonesty, misrepresentation, and trickery enter into their business dealings, and their wealth is used to oppress rather than to assist others. They debase their wealth, defiling God's bounty. Those who make wrong use of God's gifts defile their houses of life, either their bodies or their circumstances, and "God will destroy [them]" (1 Cor. 3:17).

Many people cannot stand prosperity. They lead steady, useful lives until they begin to demonstrate wealth, and then they are thrown off balance. This lack of balance may become evident in wastefulness and extravagance. This is idle use of money, heedless, thoughtless use. Everything in God's kingdom is to be used intelligently. Even Jesus told his Apostles to "Gather up the fragments left over" (Jn. 6:12) when he had more food on hand than was necessary for the feeding of the multitude. Logically, those fragments were put to some good use, else they would not have been gathered up.

All nature teaches balance. Nothing in it is ever wasted. Nature produces most lavishly, but that which is unused in the human or the animal kingdom disintegrates and returns to the soil, enriching it for the production of future harvests. If we take a lesson from nature, it is clear that balanced use of wealth demands that waste and extravagance be eliminated.

Allowing wealth to be an excuse for laziness is another way of debasing it. Any use of wealth that hinders the soul's progress is an idle or evil use. A few years ago a young man was involved in a lawsuit for an inheritance. It was a sizable inheritance that would have enabled him to live in comfort, even luxury, the rest of his life. The inheritance was justly his, but a number of false claims were made on it. Although he was a Truth student, receiving spiritual aid through prayer, the case failed to come to a quick and satisfactory conclusion. Through one technicality after another, it dragged on. It was a puzzling situation. One day, after a period of prayerful treatment for the manifestation of divine justice, his teacher asked him, "What are you going to do when this case is settled and you have the use of this fortune?" His instant answer was: "Oh, boy! First I am going around the world, and then I am never going to do another bit of work as long as I live!"

From his answer, it was evident that there was divine protection for him in the fact that the case had dragged on for so long. He was doing well in a line of work that held great possibilities for him and that, if followed, would bring out his latent talents and help him to develop a well-rounded, useful life. He was helped to see what a definite disadvantage the money would be to him until he had reconstructed his whole attitude toward it. He soon grasped the idea that money is a form of manifestation of God's limitless supply and that, to be of value to the individual, it must be used in a way becoming to the divine abundance that it symbolizes. When he received the inheritance, he remembered his lesson and became a wise steward of God's bounty; consequently his money was a blessing to himself and others.

It is a mistake to think of money as the root of all evil. The biblical passage from which this metaphor is taken states that it is the *love* of money that is the root of evil, not the money itself. Furthermore, Jesus never said that a rich man could not enter the kingdom of heaven, as is popularly supposed. What he really said was that it would be hard for a rich man to enter the kingdom of heaven.

Jesus had a number of rich men among his friends and followers, men who were honest and upright. These men were earnestly seeking to understand and obey God's will. Among them was one whom Matthew describes as "a rich man from Arimathea, named Joseph, who was also a disciple of Jesus" (Mt. 27:57). Mark, Luke, and John all speak in the highest terms of Joseph of Arimathea, who received Jesus' body from the Cross and placed it in his own new tomb hewn out of solid rock. Nowhere in the record is there any criticism of this man because of his wealth. We find him accepted without question as a follower or disciple of Jesus. Luke speaks of him as "a good and righteous man" (Lk. 23:50).

Another wealthy and influential follower of Jesus was Nicodemus, who came to him by night seeking understanding of God and His kingdom. Nicodemus was a member of the Sanhedrin, the governing body of the Jews. Undoubtedly, his wealth and influence saved him from their wrath when he defended Jesus against them. Neither of these men allowed their wealth to stand in the way of their goodness and justice.

Nowhere in the Scriptures do we find condemnation of wealth as such, only condemnation of the wrong use of wealth and of its evil effects on some people. We know that on one occasion Jesus refused to accept a certain rich young man as one of his followers, yet we also know that he did accept Joseph of Arimathea. Why? Because one was a slave to his wealth and the other was master of it. Joseph knew how to use it in God's service. He knew himself to be a steward of God's bounty. He administered his wealth wisely and well. He did not debase it by using it for idle or evil purposes. He kept it in circulation by serving God and humanity.

Jesus knew that wealth is everyone's divine heritage. He knew that God is the source of all wealth and that when we realize that God's is the ownership and ours the stewardship, and conduct ourselves accordingly, wealth can teem with spiritual blessings. He also knew, and from this knowledge he sounded his warning, that when people mix their thoughts of wealth with thoughts of lust, selfishness, extravagance, waste, and laziness, they adulterate God's good and keep themselves from enjoying happiness and harmony in the use of it.

Wealth is a symbol of God's abundance, and as such it is a blessing. When used in a way appropriate to the divine source from which it comes, we can truly say: "The blessing of the Lord makes rich, and he adds no sorrow with it" (Prov. 10:22).

Those who understand this obey prosperity's seventh commandment:

You shall not abase your wealth to idle or evil uses.

QUESTION HELPS

1. What essential Truth is incorporated in this commandment?

2. What was Jesus' teaching concerning this commandment?

3. How is the seventh commandment related to the first three?

4. How may we apply the essential idea of this commandment to our financial affairs?

5. What thoughts defile the mind and lead to wrong use of God's wealth?

6. What are some of the common ways of misusing money? What are the results of such misuse?

7. Why are some people unable to stand prosperity?

8. Is money the "root of all kinds of evil"?

9. Did Jesus require all his followers to give up their worldly possessions?

10. What is wealth when rightly understood?

THE EIGHTH COMMANDMENT

You shall not seek something for nothing.

"You shall not steal."
—Exodus 20:15

The eighth commandment, like all the others, covers a broad field of human activities. Its meaning can by no means be confined to the mere act of committing petty or grand larceny. To *steal*, according to Webster, means "to take ... without right or leave and with intent to keep ... wrongfully." Many self-righteous people believe that if they do not gain possession of another's property unlawfully they are not disobeying the eighth commandment. They condemn the misguided burglar, pickpocket, or embezzler, and as a rule are most insistent that these criminals be severely punished. This sharp intolerance of the weaknesses of others is characteristic of those who keep the letter of the law but violate its spirit.

What is the spirit of the law in "You shall not steal"? Emerson's essay "Compensation" affords several excellent answers to this question. In the last analysis, stealing is the endeavor to get something for nothing. Under the "law of compensation," this is impossible. Life, functioning under this law of Mind, demands that we pay for what we get, and it is correspondingly true that we get what we pay for. Emerson says: "In labor as in life there can be no cheating. The thief steals from himself. The swindler swindles himself."

Speaking of the man who tries to get something for nothing, he also says: "Has he gained by borrowing, through indolence or cunning, his neighbor's wares, or horses, or money? There arises on the deed the instant acknowledgment of the benefit on the one part and of debt on the other; that is, of superiority and inferiority."

"A wise man will extend this lesson to all parts of life, and know that it is the part of prudence to face every claimant and pay every just demand on your time, your talents, or your heart. Always pay; for first or last, you must pay your entire debt.... The benefit we receive must be rendered again, line for line, deed for deed, cent for cent, to somebody."

Under the law of compensation there is no such thing as getting something for nothing. We must give full measure for all that we receive at some time. Every day is a day of judgment in which the balance between giving and receiving is struck. Every instant of time, the state of mind, body, and circumstances shows just where we stand, just how well or how poorly we have observed the spirit of this commandment. Like all Truth, it is to be observed in the handling of our material supply. Prosperity's eighth commandment is:

You shall not seek something for nothing.

One of the most difficult things in life to understand is the apparently unjust distribution of riches. Self-respecting, upright people with keen minds, who are endeavoring to live constructive, creative lives, are often poor as the proverbial church mouse. Such people frequently become embittered wondering why persons who are unsound ethically, have undeveloped minds, and lead useless and sometimes vicious lives are literally rolling in manifest wealth.

The answer is that wealth is the manifestation of the state of mind. The earnestly striving person whose efforts are not richly compensated may have a poverty consciousness. This is by far the most common reason for inadequate returns for conscientious endeavor. The mind that is filled with fear of lack, acceptance of lack, or rebellion against circumstances is, for the time being, failing to collect the just compensation due in this outer realm of cause and effect. Since nothing is ever lost, such persons will reap the benefit of every effort they make when they have freed their minds from the poverty complex. On the other hand, apparently useless people who seem to be giving nothing to life

may have a money consciousness. They may be
utterly convinced that the world is their oyster and
thoughtlessly proceed to grab and use selfishly
everything in sight. With no thought of lack in
mind, they will continue wealthy, although wrong
use of wealth must eventually bring them misery
and disappointment. Such situations call for com-
passion rather than envy or rebellion, for we are
seeing only in part. We are seeing the beginning of
a violation of the law of giving and receiving that
can only result in disaster at some future time for
those who face life so unintelligently.

Those who endeavor to face life intelligently and
still find themselves poverty-stricken may be laboring under karmic law. Karma is an Oriental name
for the results of the working of the law of cause
and effect. It is sometimes used to designate the law
itself but more commonly as a name for the consequences of the violation of that law. In one of its
aspects, karma may be called a "hangover" of unful-
filled obligations, a reaping of the result of failing
to keep a balance between giving and receiving.
Whenever, in this existence or in a previous existence, a person has reached out to take something
for which he or she has given nothing in return, he
or she is bound sooner or later to find him- or herself in the position of giving but not receiving, until
the balance is restored. The law of karma, or cause
and effect, is always transcended by the law of

grace. Always remember that the law of grace is the action of Spirit of the "free gift" of God's saving power responding to the call of faith. Bewildered people who find themselves in the position of giving their best and receiving no adequate return need to learn to accept God as the only source of supply. They must covenant in their own hearts to continue serving God by giving their best to the world in confident expectation of divine fulfillment of every need. Such a "willingly giving" state of mind constitutes true repentance for those past violations of law that they may have already forgotten. They will find themselves lifted out of the net of karmic difficulties through their spirit of service and their faith. Under the law of grace, every need is freely provided for, but we must give of our wisdom, love, and effort to handle intelligently that which the grace of God so freely supplies. Give we must, either before or after receiving.

If we do not like what we are getting out of life, we must consider carefully what we are giving to life. If we feel that we cannot afford to be charitable and that we hate to pay debts, we are withholding our generosity, and life will not be generous to us.

We can always give in proportion to what we have, no matter how little it may be at any given time. If we do not have ten dollars to give, we can always find a place where ten cents can be of value, and we can give it cheerfully and with utter

confidence that since we are obeying God's law,
that law will prosper us.

When we think we are getting something for
nothing, we are self-deceived. Sometime, somewhere, somehow, we pay for everything we receive.
The following true story illustrates this fact in an
amusing way. A woman with numerous relatives
loved to travel and boasted that she never paid a
hotel bill in a city where she had relatives. "What
are relatives good for if you can't use them?" she
was often heard to say. Her method was to descend
on them bag and baggage, taking it for granted
they would be glad to see her. She would chuckle
over the fact that she was never called on to return
their hospitality because she lived in a single room
in a hotel. The amount of money she saved on
hotel bills in her travels was one of her favorite top-
ics of conversation. But another frequent topic was
the way people always tried to take advantage of
her financially. She always had to pay top price for
everything; salespeople always overcharged her.
Even fate seemed to be against her, for if she went
downtown and purchased a dress for seventy-five
dollars, that same style of dress would be put on
sale the very next day for fifty-two fifty! She was
both astonished and indignant when told that she
was violating God's law of compensation, which
requires that we give generously for all that we
receive. It was a new and not very welcome idea

that there was a definite connection between the way she treated her relatives and the way other people treated her.

Jesus emphasized the necessity of giving either before or after receiving when he said: "Give, and it will be given to you" (Lk. 6:38), and "Freely ye have received, freely give" (Mt. 10:8 KJV).

Obedience to these instructions of Jesus constitutes obedience to prosperity's eighth commandment and will keep us out of debt. If we run up bills by taking and using that for which we do not or cannot pay, we are violating this commandment as definitely as does the pickpocket, the confidence man, or the burglar.

We may claim as much as we are capable of accepting of God's bountiful supply. This is a transaction in mind, and we must proceed to substantiate our claims in the realm of form. This is demonstration. For instance, if we desire a new car and we have faith that it is the Father's goodwill that we have it, we must show our faith by our works; that is, we must demonstrate either the money to pay for it or the ability to earn the money. In other words, we have no right to take something in the realm of form when we have only our undemonstrated faith to pay for it in the realm of mind. We must give for value received in such a way that the one from whom we receive is satisfied.

Nature offers us a striking lesson on this subject.

Many abandoned farms tell the sad story of an acreage ruthlessly robbed of its values. The barren soil has been so continually cultivated that it can no longer yield a crop. Heavy rains have washed away valuable topsoil because nothing has been done to prevent it. There is no timber on the land because the trees were cut down for various purposes and none have ever been planted in their place. Such farms need never have been reduced to such a state, had their owners understood that they could not expect to get something for nothing. The soil should have been given proper resting periods; cover crops should have been put in and plowed under to enrich the soil that had given so freely to previous crops. Trees should have been planted when old ones were cut down. The valuable topsoil should have been protected. If all these things had been wisely done, many of these deserted farms would have continued supporting their owners indefinitely. In the realm of natural law, as in the realm of mind, we find constant proof of the need to keep a balance between giving and receiving.

Balanced compensation is a necessary part of the foundation of permanent prosperity. The justice of this divine law is self-evident. Wise people never seek to evade it. They know that life itself is a gift from God, and they take care to use it in a way becoming to its inherent nature, becoming far more concerned with giving than with getting. They place their neighbors' interests before their own, because they have evolved spiritually to the point where they no longer have any inclination to trick, cheat, or steal. Emerson sums up our spiritual progress along this particular line as follows: "Every man takes care that his neighbor shall not cheat him. But a day comes when he begins to care that he does not cheat his neighbor. Then all goes well. He has changed his market-cart into a chariot of the sun." He has learned to obey prosperity's eighth commandment:

You shall not seek something for nothing.

QUESTION HELPS

1. What is stealing from the worldly viewpoint? From the spiritual viewpoint?

2. Explain the law of compensation.

3. What is the inevitable result of trying to get something for nothing?

4. What is the essential Truth of the eighth commandment? How is it related to prosperity?

5. Why is every day a day of judgment?

6. Why is it that some intelligent, religious people are not prosperous?

7. How may the law of grace be called into operation to transcend the law of karma?

8. What is the relation between giving and getting? What did Jesus say about it?

9. How much of God's supply can we claim?

10. What is meant by balanced compensation?

THE NINTH COMMANDMENT

You shall not bear false witness against the source of your wealth.

"You shall not bear false witness against your neighbor."
—Exodus 20:16

The ninth commandment has to do with the essential nature of truthfulness. To "bear false witness" is to be untruthful, and any intent to deceive is a violation of this commandment. One who conscientiously observes it in the letter may still be violating the spirit of it.

The person who takes pride in never telling a deliberate lie but who cleverly manages to convey false impressions is not only untruthful but dishonest. Taking pride in a virtue that we do not possess, we are dishonest with ourselves. Exaggeration, insinuation, detraction are all forms of conveying false impressions. Even listening to gossip is bearing false witness, because it means being receptive to false things and possibly perpetuating them. Any acceptance and assertion of evil is falsifying. Stating that our neighbor is ill and discussing his or her symptoms is bearing false witness unless we also acknowledge the Christ life within him or her.

111

Affirming to others that he or she is poor or unsuccessful or involved in debt or disaster of any kind is bearing false witness against God's Truth in the situation.

All that we call evil in this realm of form is a mute testimonial to the devil, the father of lies, in our consciousness. Peter referred to the devil as the "adversary," that which is adverse to God's good, therefore the great lie, because there is no absence of that good. Jesus described the devil as the "tempter," that which in consciousness tempts us to believe in the false and to assert it. In yielding to the tempter, we accept the evidence of our senses and fail to stand fast on the Truth of God's presence. In so doing, we disobey prosperity's ninth commandment:

You shall not bear false witness against the source of your wealth.

Our earthly existence is a strange paradox. We are changeless beings moving in a realm of constantly changing conditions. We are God's image and likeness, a triumph of spiritual perfection, often moving amid conditions of sin, disease, poverty, and death. These conditions exist in our sense realm as self-evident facts, having no existence apart from the false beliefs that they embody. We call such conditions evil. Every evil is an embodiment of a false belief in the mind of an individual or an accumulation of false beliefs in what is known as the race mind.

Mind is creative of nature, and thought is its action. Through the process of thought, mind projects its ideas into the realm of form. When the ideas generated in mind are true to the spiritual power that enables us to be, to think, and to act, they appear in the realm of form in ways that make for peace of mind, health of body, and abundant well-being in circumstances, which are the "extended body." The root word of *circumstance* means that which "stands around" or encompasses. Just as our thoughts affect our bodies for good or ill, even so their far-reaching influence determines the nature of the conditions that surround us. Psychological research reveals that thought action operates under certain established laws of the mental realm that are amazingly similar to laws operating in the physical realm. As a result of the operation of these laws of mind, we find that our bodies and circumstances are the inevitable manifestation of our thought action. We may think of them as our solidified thought, as thought condensed into form.

Our thought is indicative of the way we are seeing things. Jesus said, "If your eye is healthy, your whole body will be full of light" (Mt. 6:22). He was telling us in his poetically powerful way that if we keep our thoughts focused on God and God's presence, we will be holding in mind only that which is true. Therefore our "whole body" (mind, body, and circumstances) will be "full of light"; in other words, there will be no shadow of evil, nothing false, in our lives.

Every time we say, "I am poor," we are failing to keep our thought single on the Truth of God's presence. In His presence is the fullness of supply for every need. Every time we talk about poverty, we bear false witness against God, for we deny God's presence; we are definitely stating that there is an absence of the presence of God in our lives. We know this cannot be true, so instead of bearing false witness against God, we should courageously face the condition in the positive knowledge that it is not true and has no place in our circumstances, which are impregnated with God's presence. Quietly and persistently, we should proceed to overcome evil with good by keeping our thoughts centered on God's omnipresence and goodwill for us. We should also follow Jesus' instructions and make a secret transaction with God in which we accept gladly, praisefully, the particular gift we are asking for at the moment. "And your Father who sees in secret will reward you" (Mt. 6:4). All the laws in God's universe of law are immediately operative on our unquestioningly accepting God's good, with the inevitable result of giving form to this good.

Remember that it takes two to carry out a gift

transaction. There must be a giver and a receiver, one who offers and one who accepts. Until that which is offered as a gift is accepted, there is no consummation of the transaction. Through His very presence within us and all around us, God offers us eternal life, with all its inherent perfection. At any period of our existence we manifest as much or as little as we are willing to accept of God.

Jesus instructed us not to resist evil but to overcome it with good. At the same time he was positive in his injunction that we must resist the devil. There is no conflict between these two statements. The devil is the tempter, the adversary, the temptation in our own minds to think in ways that are the adverse of God's good. Every such thought bears false witness against God. It is a lie, and as such, it must be resisted. We must say as Jesus said, "Get behind me, Satan!" (Mt. 16:23) In this way, we turn our backs on it, and it fades away into the limbo of forgotten things, while we press forward, eagerly reaching toward God's good. When we accept lack of any good thing, we bear false witness against God. We deny both God's omnipresence and goodwill. We accept certain things as facts that should be declared untrue. The average person confuses facts with Truth. Webster defines a fact as "an actual occurrence."

A fact, we might say, may be "true" or "false." The finding of a wrong answer to a problem in arithmetic is a fact, but the wrong answer itself is recognized as a "false" fact. So we erase it and make every effort to find the right answer to the problem. Every appearance of lack is a "false" fact and as such should be vigorously denied. Denial is the erasing action of mind. When we refuse to accept a "false" fact, we have taken the first step toward erasing it from our consciousness. The next step is to fill the mind with faith in God's omnipresence and good-will, knowing that whatever we hold in mind must inevitably find its way into form.

When we bear witness to the Truth of God's presence and power in our daily lives, we refuse to accept any appearances of lack or limitation. We declare firmly that they are not God's goodwill for us and that they have no part nor place in our lives. We recognize them for what they are, mistakes made in working a problem of supply, mistakes caused by blindness or ignorance on our part or on the part of others. As in every problem, there is a principle involved. The vital steps in solving the problem are to see the mistake, erase it, and then try to get the right answer by going back to principle.

In every problem of supply, the Truth that God is the one Source is the principle involved. To work out the problem of supply correctly so that plenty and not lack is the answer, we must make intelligent use of our understanding of God as principle.

We must prayerfully acknowledge God as the source of all good and declare the Truth of God's presence and power in all our circumstances; we must gratefully accept the fulfillment of our hearts' desires and staunchly declare that God's goodwill is now done in our lives. This is bearing witness unto Truth.

We must learn to be true witnesses of God's abundance not only for ourselves but for others. All around us we see the dire effects of the belief that poverty is inevitable. As long as this belief persists, there will always be those who need our help. To refuse to help on the grounds that there is no such thing as poverty, and therefore to refuse to recognize it, is placing ourselves in the class with those of whom it has been said that "a little learning is a dangerous thing." With true understanding, we learn to keep a balance between the unseen and the seen and to meet appearances of lack on both the mental and material planes. While we deny the false causal belief, we are quick to render material assistance where we know it can be of benefit and not contribute to the weakness or laziness of the individual. We should contribute to public charities and work for the alleviation of suffering, but always clearly holding to the truth that God never ordered it so, that we are simply clearing up our mistakes.

No matter how false the appearance may be, we can always tell the truth about God. When we stop bearing false witness against God and start acknowledging His presence as the "answering substance" ever ready to fulfill our every need, we will be blessed with abundant good. Learn to speak directly to God's ever-waiting presence:

"Dear Father-Mother God, in Your presence within me and all around me is the abundance of all good. It is Your goodwill that Your abundant good be expressed through me. I am free from the fear of lack because of Your riches within. Your limitless wealth is mine. I receive it in faith and disburse it in love and wisdom. You are my rich Father-Mother, and I am Your rich child living in Your rich world."

Such acknowledgements as these in the face of any appearance to the contrary constitute obedience to the ninth commandment:

You shall not bear false witness against the source of your wealth.

QUESTION HELPS

1. What are some ways of violating the spirit of this commandment?

2. What is the devil?

3. What is the essential Truth of this commandment? How may it be applied in establishing prosperity?

4. Explain the paradox of earthly existence.

5. How are body and circumstances related to our thoughts?

6. Why is there no contradiction between the biblical injunctions: "Do not resist an evildoer" (Mt. 5:39) and "Resist the devil" (Jas. 4:7)?

7. Explain the difference between "fact" and "Truth."

8. How should appearances of lack be treated?

9. What is the principle involved in every problem of supply?

10. How may we bear witness to Truth?

THE TENTH
COMMANDMENT

You shall not limit yourself by coveting that which is another's; you shall claim your own.

"You shall not covet your neighbor's house; you shall not covet your neighbor's wife, or male or female slave, or ox, or donkey, or anything that belongs to your neighbor."
—Exodus 20:17

In the tenth commandment, "You shall not covet," Moses reaches a sweeping climax in which he passes from the realm of effects to the realm of causes. The first four commandments have to do with right action toward God, the last six with right action toward other human beings. Interpreted according to the letter of the law, right action toward others begins with filial service. Right action toward the rest of the world demands that we shall not kill, commit adultery, steal, or lie. All these are transactions in the outer realm of action. The tenth commandment, "You shall not covet," has to do solely with transactions in the inner realm of mind.

It would appear on the surface that the tenth commandment is something in the nature of an anticlimax: killing, adultery, stealing, and lying seem so much more serious than coveting. The understanding mind, however, realizes that covetousness is the mental cause from which the outer effects of lying, stealing, adultery, and killing emanate. Following the example of Jesus, we, too, may draw an illustration from nature and call covetousness the mental soil in which weed ideas germinate and eventually blossom forth, bearing fruit of an evil nature.

Covetousness is always the cause of stealing and adultery. The inordinate desire for that which belongs to another culminates in these two evils. Covetousness is also largely responsible for lying and killing, although other causes frequently enter into these two violations of law. Finally, much unkind and unjust treatment of parents is bred of a covetous state of mind. Shakespeare dramatizes this particular aspect of covetousness in his tragedy, *King Lear.* Having yielded his wealth and power to his covetous and "marblehearted" daughters, King Lear finds himself "a poor, infirm, weak, and despised old man," and cries out in the agony of his soul, "How sharper than a serpent's tooth it is to have a thankless child."

The cause of covetousness is our failure to look to God as the source of our supply. We see something and want it and, in that wanting, fail to realize that the ever-present "goodwilling" Power will supply it to us through our faith. We make the mistake of thinking that what we see in the realm of form is the only possible fulfillment of our desire. We do not know—or we forget—that the power of supply is limitless and that the same form can be reproduced endlessly at the demand of faith. When we covet, we limit ourselves because of our false belief that God is unable to supply us with our hearts' desires. Every covetous thought is fundamentally a belief that there is not enough to go around. When we place our faith in God as the source of our prosperity, we can rejoice in the good of others, because we realize that there is plenty more for us. We have learned to obey prosperity's tenth commandment:

You shall not limit yourself by coveting that which is another's; you shall claim your own.

Covetousness is desire misinterpreted. Desire is a potent factor in the creative process. It is the initial step. In H. Emilie Cady's *Lessons in Truth*, we find this statement: "Desire for anything is the thing itself in incipiency." We can never truly desire anything that cannot exist for us. We may wish for absurd or impossible things, but we cannot desire them, for desire is insistent yearning, and anything the heart yearns for insistently is possible to attain. We are told in the Old Testament, "As he [man] thinketh in his heart, so is he" (Prov. 23:7 KJV). In modern language, we should say that we are just what we feel ourselves to be; we are manifestations of the sum total of our inner yearnings or desires. We may be manifestations of our frustrated desires. In our ignorance of God's law, we may see the fulfillment of our desires in the possessions of another person and suffer under the illusion that another has what we want. This is not true, for only God has what we want, and God delivers it to us on the call of our faith. Desire is always the first indication of some good that God has for us. When we wrap it in the pall of covetousness and bury it in the tomb of ignorance, it fails to materialize.

Have you ever watched two baby chicks struggling for the possession of a good, stout worm? In the freshly spaded soil, there are plenty of worms, but the chicks are blind to the feast around them because they can both see only one worm. Along comes a larger chicken who not only takes the worm away from them but also drives them from the scene of the feast. This is a good illustration of many a situation in the realm of human affairs. Often while we are intent on striving to wrest something we want from another, the entire situation changes and someone else steps in and gets the prize. When we use good judgment, we never fall into the error of believing that we can fulfill our hearts' desires only by taking something from another. We know that such ignorant action is bred of a lack of understanding of God's omnipresent substance, the limitless spiritual substance or energy that fills all thought forms and manifests itself accordingly.

To understand this better, let us borrow an illustration from the realm of natural law. An electrical engineer knows how to generate energy by conforming to the laws governing electricity. This energy can be converted into innumerable forms, such as light, heat, and power, according to the conditions furnished by the engineer. The metaphysician knows that Divine Mind, which is living intelligence, has already created the energy that we convert into the forms we desire. This energy is the omnipresent spiritual substance that is always ready to respond to the call of faith. Being a mind force, it needs only the action of our minds as an instrument for its functioning. Faith furnishes the absolutely right conditions under which God's spiritual substance, which Emerson calls the primal energy, moves in resistless power to make manifest the thing desired.

Sometimes an electrical engineer may get into grave difficulties through short circuits. Short circuits are caused by some interference that creates wrong conditions. This is true electrically and mentally. When God's energy is flowing through our faith toward the manifesting of a desired goal, all extraneous conditions must be met in the right way if short circuits are to be avoided. One of the most common ways of short-circuiting mentally is to allow the thought of interference on the part of another personality to disrupt our faith. Where such a condition arises, we must preserve our faith by holding fast to that which we know to be true. Our mental attitude toward others must be that everything real, constructive, creative, and powerful in them, the Christ Self, desires and is working only for God's goodwill for us. Then we can look on any seemingly antagonistic outer action with serenity, feeling that these things move us not, because we know that all things work together for our good.

Covetousness is another sure way of short-circuiting the spiritual energy on its way to mani-festation. Again faith, the necessary condition of mind permitting God's energy to move, is dis-rupted by the transferring of attention from God's limitless supply to someone's material possessions.

Belief in divine supply remedies all such mis-takes, and the supply is delivered into form, through faith, according to the pattern of the desire. When this spiritual principle is understood, we no longer covet; we rejoice instead in our neigh-bor's good fortune, because we see it as an evidence of God's bounty. We continue to rejoice, knowing that this same bounty is ours for our acceptance. Through our faith, the equivalent of our neighbor's good can appear in our own lives. It may not be identical in appearance, but it will be the same good adapted to our needs in such a way as to bring us the greatest joy.

Faith is the starting point. Poised in faith, the soul becomes the instrument of God's action. Infinite wisdom guides and directs us whether or not we are aware of it. Divine love protects us and serves as a great magnet, drawing to us whatever is necessary for the fulfillment of our hearts' desires. The limitless power of the spiritual energy of the universe brings all things, on all planes, together for the reciprocal working out of the desire. Faith is our contribution in any situation where desire is involved. God does the rest.

The hidden Truth in this commandment is that we are to cease limiting ourselves by desiring that which is another's. We are to learn how to claim our own from the one divine Source of supply.

You shall not limit yourself by coveting that which is another's; you shall claim your own.

We all desire what is known as a prosperity consciousness. We know that such a consciousness establishes us in a state of permanent prosperity. In each of the ten commandments, we have found an injunction that must be observed if we are to live in the freedom of plenty. Out of these instructions, we may evolve ten powerful affirmations:

1. *I look only to God for my prosperity.*
2. *I make no mental images of lack.*
3. *I speak no word of limitation.*
4. *I let go and let God work in my affairs.*
5. *I deal honorably with God and all God's pay clerks.*
6. *I keep my wealth circulating wisely.*
7. *I use my wealth for good purposes only.*
8. *I never strive to get something for nothing.*
9. *I never talk poverty; I tell the Truth about God's abundance.*
10. *I take my eye off my neighbor's wealth; I claim my own!*

In these affirmations, we have the essence of *Prosperity's Ten Commandments.* Rightly lived, they will deliver the rich promise of our Scriptures: "The Lord will make you abound in prosperity .... The Lord will open for you his rich storehouse, the heavens ... to bless all your undertakings" (Deut. 28:11-12).

QUESTION HELPS

1. What is the relation of the tenth commandment to the nine that precede it?

2. What is the root cause of covetousness?

3. How are covetousness and limitation related?

4. How may we apply the essential Truth of this commandment to our prosperity?

5. How does covetousness impede the fulfillment of our good and just desires?

6. How do we frequently "short-circuit" the flow of our supply?

7. What should be our mental attitude toward another's prosperity?

8. How are faith and desire related?

9. What state of mind is necessary for permanent prosperity?

10. Memorize the ten prosperity affirmations.

APPENDIX A

GETTING OUT OF THE PAST

One of the most interesting bits of symbology found in the old Egyptian mythology is the story of that fabulous bird, the phoenix. According to the story, the phoenix was sacred to the god of life, Osiris, and lived a solitary life in the desert wastes. After an existence of about five hundred years, the bird, beaten and buffeted, old and worn, tired of existence, would make of its nest a funeral pyre, and, settling down amid the flames, would be completely consumed. Then, wonder of wonders, from the pile of ashes would burst forth in all its pristine glory a new phoenix; new life, power, and beauty out of the ashes of the old. You can readily see why the phoenix was the emblem of immortality to the ancient Egyptians and why today we use the word *phoenix* to typify new growth springing from old ruins.

Have you ever thought how phoenixlike is our existence on this earthly plane? How we, like the phoenix, at times rise from the ruins, the ashes, of some phase of our existence to a higher, finer, nobler expression of life? Only, unlike that mythical bird, we do not deliberately destroy existing conditions in order to set ourselves free. Far from it; we usually face with horror and dismay the seeming disaster closing in on us—too material-minded, too short of vision, to see that only through the seeming disaster can we attain freedom from the clutch of circumstance, which is choking our fuller, finer expression. When someone goes through seeming ruin in the realm of finance or perhaps the emotional realm of love and harmony or the realm of health and comes through the ordeal better and finer, less material-minded and more spiritual-minded than before, we say that he or she has passed through a disintegration process.

There are many interesting things to be learned about this disintegration process. Oftentimes we are in a set of circumstances that, no matter how well they satisfy our material desires, fail to satisfy our soul. No matter how well our physical needs may be cared for, we have a sense of something lacking, a divine discontent. When through lack of wisdom, we fail to see our soul's need and therefore fail to satisfy it, then the material wealth and material surroundings that are blinding our true, inner vision will drop away from us. The disintegration process will set in. One by one we will lose those things which we had considered all-important and in the struggle attendant upon that loss will come face to face with our real, inner Self. Life will take on a new meaning; out of the ashes of the old, the new self will rise, and we will build again, more truly, more firmly, more lastingly, than before. People will say of us, "Why, they're not the same at all." We are not. The old self has passed away in that general disintegration process, and the new self that has risen from the ruins is nearer our real Self—a better expression of the indwelling Christ.

Concrete examples sometimes help us to get an idea firmly established. Let me give you one. Let me tell you of a family who a few years ago was living a life of ease and comfort. Each member had plenty of the world's goods, yet slowly but surely the higher vision of each was growing dimmed. They were people who had started in life together with little else than the benefits of good home environment and good education. Gradually, in the course of years, they had accumulated plenty of material comforts. They had grown in worldly wealth, but they had shrunk spiritually. They had at first kept their minds keen with good reading and by keeping in close touch with matters of current interest, but with the growth of material wealth, they even allowed their minds to become stagnant. The husband no longer read anything but that which had a direct bearing on his business. The wife found no time for anything but the new fiction. They no longer enjoyed the close mental companionship bred of reading, enjoying, and discussing books together. They drifted apart—the wife immersed in her social interests, the husband in his business, and the children were left in the care of servants. There was no longer a beautiful family life of mutual interests, and seemingly no way of reestablishing it. Discontented, vaguely unhappy, really yearning for a higher expression of life, they went on in a virtual treadmill, and what happened? Business disasters fell thick and fast, and one short year found them not only penniless but heavily in debt. It was all seemingly terrible and bewildering. Why should they, who had always lived upright, honest lives, have become victims of such unavoidable disaster—so involved in the "fell clutch of circumstance"? Then as they faced the ruins came the great illumination; they were closer in spirit than they had been for years. The scales fell from their eyes; they found their real Self, and, phoenixlike, they rose from the ruins and built a surer, firmer, truer foundation on which to start anew.

This is but one example of the great disintegration process that we see going on all around us, and that we sometimes face in our own experience. When the soul yearns for that which existing circumstances deny it, forces will be set into operation to disintegrate those circumstances and free the inner man or woman to build anew.

Unfortunately, we fail sometimes to see this sweeping away of the old as but a means toward the end of rebuilding the new. Instead of rising, phoenixlike, with renewed life, strength, and courage, we stand amid the ruins of the past and bind ourselves to those ruins with the chains of regret. There is nothing so hampering to progress as regret. Do you remember the story of Lot's wife? How many of us are pillars of salt? How many of us are turning the fertile soil of our mind into an arid, desolate waste by constantly watering it with the salty tears of regret? As long as we live in the past, we can make no progress in the now, and it is the ever present, eternal now that is all-important to us. The past means nothing in our life save as it has made us what we are now. The only value that any experience in our past has for us is in the lesson that it teaches us. If we have learned that lesson, then we are through with that experience; it has no further place in our life. We become the living testimonial of that lesson learned. There is no need of going over it again. But if we have failed to learn the lesson of some previous experience, then be sure that we shall have to live through a similar experience and perhaps another and another until we do learn the lesson. The lesson once learned, the experience is blotted out so far as we are concerned, and the lesson that it taught—the new wisdom, the new judgment, the new tolerance—is ours in the now and serves as a guide while we build anew.

We sometimes find it difficult to get out of the past because we are so weighed down with bad habits. We all want to head our train of life toward the goal of better living, and we know that for speed we must unload all unnecessary baggage.

Have you ever watched a heavily loaded freight train getting under way? It uses an enormous amount of power in starting, and when it finally moves, it creeps at a snail's pace—except on the downgrades. There it travels rapidly enough, but oh, the effort that goes into making the upgrade! The train of life proceeds in much the same way. When our life is heavily burdened with bad habits of thought and action and much that is nonessential, we are like the heavily loaded freight train, using up power and squandering energy and making slow progress except on the downgrades. Here, unfortunately, the very weight of that extra baggage we are carrying rushes us along into situations and problems from which we find it exceedingly difficult to pull out to continue our journey.

How may we unload? We have tried many a time by making what we called good resolutions. Spiritually considered, there is a right way and a wrong way to make a resolution. To say "I will not do thus and so" is the wrong way. It is the way of "won't" power. Only our personal will is behind such a declaration, and that is weak at best. The right way to overcome the weakness is by relying upon the unfailing strength of divine will, to affirm that God's goodwill is now operative in our life.

If we wish to drop our load of bad habits, let us waste no time on declarations like this: "I will not smoke too much, drink too much, eat too much, talk too much"—as the case may be. Instead, let us sturdily affirm: *I am temperate in all ways because I am a child of God.* With fervor and persistency, let us then image ourselves acting in all ways as becomes a child of God. With this image of our own right action will come the corresponding image of the peace and happiness and deep content that of necessity is the fruit of such action. Let us no more declare, "I will not gossip, I will not criticize," but, instead, affirm constantly and with deepest conviction: *I am loving in all ways because I am a child of God.* What a joy to think of oneself as a loving child of God! The bit of scandal dies on the lips; the criticism dissolves, like ice in the warm glow of the sun, before it is ever voiced.

Would you unload the habit of extravagance? Then assert the Truth: *I am discriminating in all ways because I am a child of God.* A person of discrimination is never extravagant or wasteful. In every instance, we find that we can drop our load of bad habits by strengthening those qualities in the soul which need strengthening. Any other method is merely putting a new patch on an old garment, and Jesus Christ taught us that there is no lasting good in such patchwork. Bad habits of the flesh can only be overcome through building spiritual values into the soul.

Are you carrying a load of animosities? Nothing weighs heavier or is more effectual in retarding your progress toward better and more successful living than old grudges, petty jealousies, a sense of injury or self-pity, or anything else that may come under the head of animosity. Remember always that the burden rests more heavily on the one who condemns than on the one condemned.

Above all, drop your load of regrets for past mistakes, or sins. Many a life is being lived in the shadow of such regrets. What is sin, after all, but a mistake? Taking the wrong for the right, aiming for happiness, but missing the mark. The cry in so many souls is, "If I could only undo it, if I could only begin over!" You can never undo what you have done, but you can always make what you have done a power for spiritual uplift rather than a power for discouragement and despondency. If in answer to the question, "Would I under any circumstances commit that sin again?" you can with all the strength of your soul say, "Never, I have learned my lesson," then yours is a stronger, nobler soul than before it was tempted and fell. So why go on saying in your heart, "I am a poor, miserable sinner, and there is no good in me," when you know that nothing could induce you to sin thus again? Because you once sinned, you are not now a sinner; you are a soul made stronger by a lesson learned through a past mistake. Who is better capable of guiding a headstrong, reckless girl than one who has tasted to the bitter dregs the results of heedless folly? What man is better able to guide and influence weak-willed youth than one who has paid the penalty and learned the lesson of a mistake?

Start today changing your way of living by creating in yourself new states of mind. This can be accomplished by remembering that you are a spiritual being; by remembering that the spirit God has given you is not the spirit of weakness, fear, and doubt, but of strength, courage, and faith. Remember the words of John: "Beloved, we are God's children now" (1 Jn. 3:2). Claim your heritage; speak the word of Truth firmly: *I am a child of God, and I can do all things through His power which strengthens me.*

When you have the courage to stand firmly, with faith believing, upon the Truth of your own being, the light of understanding shines through your mind. When you are renewed in the spirit of your mind, you soon find yourself restored to better and happier ways of living. The mind that is rejoicing in its own divine heritage just naturally cannot be filled with the desire to speak unkindly or untruthfully. The glorious sense of freedom that comes with the realization of spiritual power completely shatters the bondage of fleshly appetites, and the bad habits we have acquired pass into the limbo of forgotten things.

Come out of the past; live in the now. Claim all the power, all the strength, all the growth, that is yours by virtue of your past mistakes. Get the realization that you are to:

> *Build on resolve, and not upon regret,*
> *The structure of thy future. Do not grope*
> *Among the shadows of old sins, but let*
> *Thine own soul's light shine on the path of hope*
> *And dissipate the darkness. Waste no tears*
> *Upon the blotted record of past years,*
> *But turn the leaf and smile, oh, smile, to see*
> *The fair white pages that remain to thee.*

Come out from under the shadow of self-condemnation; come forth into the light of Truth. See yourself as you really are, an expression of divine Spirit. Recognize the Christ within your soul, and in that recognition, the dead past will drop from you and you will make the ever-present now a testimonial to indwelling Spirit—to the Divine within yourself.

APPENDIX B
MIRACLE-WORKING PRAYER

Through the publicity that prayer has been receiving lately, much of the superstitious, ignorant attitude toward it is being dissipated. People are beginning to realize that prayer is simply feeling the presence of God and accepting His presence as the fulfillment of need. There is a growing understanding that all form and ritual is useless save as it impresses the mind with awareness of God. Anything that will help the mind to have faith in God's presence is of value, for mind is the only means of communing or coming into conscious union with God, and prayer is the method employed.

There are many ways of praying. Any way that produces results is good. Jesus Christ's statement "Ye shall know them by their fruits" (Mt. 7:16 KJV) may well be applied to methods of prayer. Only results prove the efficacy of the method. This we know, that anything that helps us to feel God's presence brings results. This feeling may come with a wave of emotion when we are so beaten down that we are ready to surrender to God's will, or it may come with a state of exaltation induced by some impressive religious service, or the feeling may even be aroused by the beauty of nature. Many changes of heart that have brought about outer adjustments in both body and circumstances have been the fruits of prayer in a state of exaltation. This method, however, is very uncertain. We cannot always rely on a wave of emotion or a sweep of exaltation when we seek God in prayer. What we need is an understanding of a sure method by which we can get consistently good results.

Jesus Christ gave the world such a method, a way of prayer consistently productive of good results. His instruction may be summed up in two ideas: seeking and asking. Each is half of a perfect whole; each is incomplete without the other.

Truth students oftentimes make the mistake of thinking that seeking and asking are two entirely different modes of prayer and that one has an advantage over the other. Those who accept the instruction "Strive first for the kingdom of God and his righteousness, and all these things will be given to you" (Mt. 6:33), without relating it to Jesus Christ's further instructions concerning prayer, maintain that we should never ask for *things.* They feel that asking for the fulfillment of any outer need is very materialistic and that no truly spiritual-minded person would stoop to it. Yet Jesus Christ definitely instructed us to ask for any good thing we desire, believing we receive it.

"Whatever you ask for in prayer with faith, you will receive" (Mt. 21:22).

Surely he asked for certain particular things from the Giver of all good when he performed his many miracles of healing and supply. When he fed the multitudes, he definitely had in mind loaves and fishes, for he asked what manner of food they had on hand and he took all that they had, and when "he looked up to heaven, and blessed and broke the loaves" (Mt. 14:19), he was giving thanks for that particular food and accepting from the Giver of all good gifts enough loaves and fishes to feed the entire multitude. He did not ask for manna from heaven; he did not ask that they be miraculously spared the pangs of hunger. He quite definitely asked that the few loaves and fishes on hand be multiplied to satisfy the hunger of every man, woman, and child present. He got exactly what he asked for, not only enough for the purpose but an oversupply which, knowing that there is no waste in the kingdom, he ordered gathered up in order that it might be wisely used at some future time.

Again it is reasonable to believe that when he restored sight to the blind man, he accepted perfect eyesight from the divine Source of life that he knew was ever indwelling the man. We know that he must have been thinking of eyes, because we are told of his mixing clay and spittle and placing it on the man's eyes and telling him to go and wash in the Pool of Siloam. When he told the paralytic to rise and take up his bed and walk, he must have accepted from the one Presence a strong and healthy body that could lift and carry the mat upon which the man had been lying. Before the tomb of Lazarus, he "looked upward and said, 'Father, I thank you'" (Jn. 11:41). For what? Not for eternal life for Lazarus, for he knew he already had that. In giving thanks he must have asked, believing that he was receiving, a specific thing: the reanimation of the body of Lazarus. In this instance, he spoke aloud, thanking the Father that He had heard him. What had the Father heard? Undoubtedly his soul's silent acceptance of a healthy, normally functioning physical body for Lazarus. He explains his reason for speaking aloud his thanks for the fulfillment of his desire when he says, "I knew that you always hear me, but I have said this for the sake of the crowd standing here, so that they may believe that you sent me" (Jn. 11:42). He wanted them to know that the restoration of Lazarus to earthly living was not accomplished through his personal power but by virtue of his faith in the divine Presence with which he lived in constant communion.

These instances, and many more that could be cited, are the answer to those who say that it is not spiritual to ask God for the fulfillment of our earthly needs.

On the other hand, there are many who pay little or no attention to the instruction, "Strive first for the kingdom of God," and concentrate wholly on demonstrating their supply by the method of asking. They know that to ask, believing that they receive, they must accept and that to accept any good thing means using the power of visualization and affirmation in claiming it as their own. They are so concerned with demonstrating things that their sole interest in Jesus Christ's teaching seems to be that of extracting what they believe will help them to get what they need to satisfy their material wants. Because of the operation of the mental law of suggestion as well as that of cause and effect, they meet with a modicum of success, but as a general rule, they become tense and worn out with the effort and eventually find that they are no longer successful in demonstrating.

Now those who follow exclusively the idea of seeking only the kingdom of God in prayer inevitably develop a loving, unselfish mind. They would not take anything for their new outlook on life because of the great depth of inner satisfaction they feel as they turn their thoughts to the divine Presence, but too often such people are completely bewildered because they continue in poverty or in ill-health. They fail to realize that even though they love God, their body, if diseased, will continue to present this false appearance as long as their thoughts are inactive as regards definitely accepting a strong and healthy body from the Giver of life. They also fail to realize that really to love God with all their heart is to love His presence as the fullness of all good in their circumstances, and to do that, they must definitely accept of Him the good He has for them and stop letting their thoughts accept the unfortunate appearances. The person who says, "I have faith in God and know that He will fulfill my every need," and at the same time feels that it is an insult to God to thank Him for good food and the money to pay the rent is shutting God out of the activities of his or her daily life without knowing it.

The understanding mind sees how inevitable it is that these two ideas—seeking and asking—must be the two halves of the whole of the prayer that Jesus Christ taught. Sometimes he dwelt upon one aspect and sometimes on the other. The important thing to remember is that whenever he gave specific instructions concerning the way of the complete and perfect prayer, he used both the idea of seeking and the idea of asking. With Jesus, the idea of seeking always came first, just as he said it should in the statement, "Strive first for the kingdom of God." This is entirely logical, for unless we first quiet our minds and withdraw from all thought of worldly things and dwell in meditation upon the presence of God within us and all around us, we have absolutely nothing from which we can ask, or accept, the good we desire.

The process of seeking is that of filling the mind with the realization of God's presence as the all-powerful, everywhere-present, loving wisdom that is able to do all things. The process of asking, believing that we receive, is that of identifying the particular good desired at the moment and accepting it thankfully.

Having taught in many different ways the necessity of seeking first the kingdom and then asking in faith, believing, Jesus Christ gathered his entire instruction concerning prayer into the following brief summary: "Whenever you pray, go into your room and shut the door and pray to your Father who is in secret; and your Father who sees in secret will reward you" (Mt. 6:6).

To enter into "your room" and shut the door is to withdraw into the sanctuary of one's own soul and close all avenues of thought and feeling to worldly ideas. We may do this in the midst of a crowd. More often we go apart to some chosen, quiet place where, not exposed to interruption, we may become oblivious to outer things. Jesus Christ went up into the mountains or into the wilderness or into a garden or into an "upper room." Entering into "your room" is establishing a certain state of mind; it makes no difference where the body is. When we have succeeded in withdrawing from the world both mentally and emotionally, we naturally

are concentrating thought and feeling upon those
things which are not of the world but of the kingdom of God. So once more, in the instruction to
enter into your room and shut the door, we are told
to seek the kingdom of God. Note that this instruction again comes *first*. We are then told to ask in
prayer. The promise follows that the Father who
sees (understands) in secret will reward us. There is
a striking similarity between the wording of this
instruction and the statement found in the Old
Testament "Thou shalt also decree a thing, and it
shall be established unto thee" (Job 22:28 KJV). In
both cases, we are to accept the good desired and
have faith that God, working through the laws of
His invisible realm of mind, will produce the
desired results in manifestation.

Jesus made it plain throughout his teachings that
prayer is heart action and not lip action. He
revealed that prayer is a secret transaction between
human and Divine and that mere words, no matter
how beautifully put together, can never constitute
prayer. In spite of his revelation, the disciples still
begged him to teach them to pray. He had offered
them the brimming cup of spiritual understanding
concerning prayer, but they needed a handle with
which to lay hold of it, and seeing this, He gave
them a certain formula for prayer, which we know
as the Lord's Prayer. It had far better be called the
Lord's formula for prayer. A formula is a model.

Chemically speaking, Webster describes formula as "a symbolic expression of the chemical composition or constitution of a substance." For instance, the formula for water is H_2O, meaning that water is composed of two parts of hydrogen to one of oxygen. Using this formula, a chemist can combine the elements of hydrogen and oxygen and produce water, but the formula is not the water. It is only a symbol of the water, a guide by which one who understands can produce water.

The words of the Lord's Prayer do not in themselves constitute a prayer; they constitute a formula that an understanding heart may use to fashion a productive prayer.

In the Lord's Prayer, Jesus Christ incorporated all his previous instructions concerning prayer: seeking first the kingdom and then asking the good desired, believing that you receive. The first four statements have to do with seeking, the next four with asking, and the last statement is one of acknowledgment and praise. The first statement directs our mind toward the seeking of God by reminding us of our relationship to Him and to all our human family through Him. In this same opening statement, our thoughts are also directed toward the realization that the divine Source we have just acknowledged ever indwells us: "Our Father which art in heaven" (Mt. 6:9 KJV). Remember, Jesus said that the kingdom of God is *within us.*

In the second statement, we know that "hallowed" means holy and that holy comes from a root word meaning whole: only that which is whole can be perfect or holy. We also know that the name of anything is our consciousness of the nature of that particular thing; so in the words "Hallowed be thy name," he is urging us to seek to perfect our consciousness of God's nature within us.

In the next statement, "Thy kingdom come," he instructs us to carry our consciousness of God's perfection within us into our outer living. The fourth statement, "Thy will be done in earth, as it is in heaven," guides us into the endeavor to surrender our personal will to God's goodwill for only in such surrender can the good that is ours in the invisible kingdom within us be made manifest on earth in our daily affairs.

So far the Lord's formula has been a guide enabling us to seek first the kingdom of God as we enter into prayer. It has concentrated our thought upon His might and majesty within us and all around us. In the statements that follow, Jesus Christ directs us to ask (or accept) the fulfillment of our needs of both mind and body from the Presence to whom we have addressed our thought and feeling. Each statement is what may be called a blanket statement, all-inclusive.

"Give us this day our daily bread." Right here the individual accepts from the God presence the fulfillment of his or her own particular outer need. This is in accordance with Jesus Christ's previous teaching: "If God so clothes the grass of the field, which is alive today and tomorrow is thrown into the oven, will he not much more clothe you—you of little faith?" (Mt. 6:30) Paul understood Jesus Christ's way of prayer when he said: "Rejoice in the Lord always; again I will say, Rejoice.... The Lord is at hand. Have no anxiety about anything, but in everything by prayer and supplication with thanksgiving let your requests be made known to God" (Phil. 4:4-6 RSV).

The next statement, "And forgive us our debts, as we forgive our debtors," has to do with establishing ourselves in peace and happiness with our neighbors by the use of God's law of love. We make our own particular application of this statement by accepting God's love in our own hearts and in the hearts of all who have anything to do with our affairs with the end in view that peace, justice, and right relationships with all may be established in our lives.

There is much controversy concerning the correct translation of the next statement, "And lead us not into temptation." One of the earliest translations into English of this particular passage was "Let us not in temptation." The word *let* used in this way means, according to *Webster's New International Dictionary*, "to leave; relinquish;

abandon." This was the common usage of the word in the sixteenth century and is still permissible. It is this translation that is accepted in the Unity rendering of the Lord's Prayer, which says, "Leave us not in temptation." The understanding heart, knowing that God never tempts us, realizes that in using this statement, we are asking (accepting) the strength and power to move in paths of righteousness; paths of right use of thought, word, and action, so that we may overcome the temptations of our own lower nature and those in the world around us.

The final asking of the Lord's formula is the acceptance of deliverance from evil. No matter what the evil appearance besetting our path, we now accept the protective power of the Almighty and know that although a thousand may fall at our side and ten thousand at our right hand, we need fear no evil, for we are following Jesus Christ and dwelling in the "secret place of the Most High," and we can safely say with the Psalmist, "My God, in whom I trust" (Ps. 91:2 RSV).

The Lord's formula, as given by Jesus Christ, closes with the final prayer of asking deliverance from evil. Most eminent authorities state that the closing line of praiseful worship commonly used is not a part of the original text, but a sort of doxology that is very ancient and was in common use in Biblical times. It was added to the prayer by the Protestant churches and incorporated in the King

James version of our Bible. It is fitting that this ancient doxology should be used as the climax—a burst of praiseful acknowledgment of the divine Source from whom the good desired has been accepted: "For thine is the kingdom, and the power, and the glory, for ever. Amen."

Seeking, asking, praising—these are all incorporated in the Lord's formula for prayer. It is Jesus Christ's way of prayer. He who chooses this way and follows it zealously finds the secret of productive prayer.

QUESTION HELPS

1. Of what value are form and ritual in prayer?

2. Is a state of exaltation induced by outer stimuli essential to prayer?

3. What are the two aspects of the perfect way of prayer taught by Jesus Christ?

4. Is there any contradiction between the two?

5. What is the relation between them?

6. What is the result of overemphasis on "asking"?

7. Why do those who concentrate only on "seeking" often fail to demonstrate health or prosperity?

8. How did Jesus Christ introduce the idea of balancing *seeking* and *asking* in his instructions on prayer?

9. Why is the Lord's Prayer a formula for all prayer? What portion has to do with "seeking"? With "asking"?

10. What is the third idea incorporated in the Lord's formula for prayer ?

ABOUT THE AUTHOR

Georgiana Tree West was born on January 18, 1882, in London, England, and was brought to the United States at a young age by her parents. An only child, she described herself as preferring to read than to play and as having too much time to read and to think alone. Raised in the Episcopal Church, she didn't find satisfying answers to her questions until, at the age of fifteen, she discovered Christian Science.

Finding stimulating answers but no emotional comfort in the cold principles she studied, Georgiana grew up and married a mining engineer, Bill West. For some years her life was hectic, living in mining camps, being constantly uprooted. Unity author Dana Gatlin wrote: "She learned to ride, shoot, and play poker, acquiring adaptability, which is one of life's biggest lessons." (See Foreword).

Adaptability was to serve her well. In six years, she had two babies and three major operations. She described herself: "I think my shifting mental state reacted on my health; some organs did not heal, and I felt very sorry for myself.... Then I got rebellious, which is a good sign! My husband had become interested in constructive thinking and was using it in his business affairs, and he thought it might help my health." Help it did, indeed. This new interest in constructive thought linked up with the spiritual principles she had studied earlier and, suddenly, she became hungry for spiritual enlightenment. She studied the eastern religions, particularly Buddhism, and theosophy and "lived with the findings of men like Emerson and Troward."

In 1924 Bill West's business took him to Louisville, Kentucky. On Easter Sunday Georgiana felt an "uncontrollable urge" to go to the Unity center in Louisville. After the service, the speaker and center leader, Rebecca Allen, asked to speak with her and then asked her to assist her as the center hostess! Soon she was taking charge of the Wednesday morning classes. Within five months she was doing full-time work at the center, and in eleven months she became the leader!

Georgiana's ministry thrived, and in eight years the center was strong and so was her health. While a graduate of the Unity Correspondence Course, she did not receive any other formal training as a speaker or a minister, yet her abilities grew along with her faith as she practiced the principles she was teaching. In 1935 she was ordained a Unity minister.

Soon another opportunity to serve arose. Ernest C. Wilson, one of the great ministers of the Unity movement, described it: "When Richard Lynch relinquished his New York City ministry to devote his energies to writing, traveling, and lecturing in the Unity field, Mrs. West was considered to be the best qualified minister available to succeed him. But for a relatively unknown minister from Louisville to attempt to replace Unity's most outstanding minister, in the country's great metropolis, was quite a challenge."

Mrs. West was up to the challenge. She decided to move the Sunday services to the Waldorf-Astoria Hotel, a risky and expensive move. Her faith and constructive thinking won out, and soon the congregation began to support the move. In 1938 Georgiana Tree West founded the Unity Center of Practical Christianity in New York City.

Between 1937 and 1948, Georgiana found herself periodically teaching at the Unity Training School in Missouri; her classes were always in demand. She also had begun to write, publishing a book, *Usable Psychology* by DeVorss, in 1929. She continued to write articles and pamphlets for Unity School and for Unity Center of Practical Christianity. In 1946 the book for which she is best known, *Prosperity's Ten Commandments*, was published by Unity Books.

Retiring from active ministry in 1957, Georgiana continued to visit and teach at Unity's headquarters at Unity Village, Missouri. In 1962 she graduated from Teacher's College in Salem, Massachusetts.

By the time Georgiana Tree West made her transition on December 15, 1974, she had demonstrated the power of spiritual principle, of constructive thought, and of faith. She was a great overcomer, overcoming considerable ill-health and physical challenge as well as growing two ministries into radiant health. Ernest C. Wilson called her "always the gracious lady, considerate of others, emanating an atmosphere of poise and serenity."

Unity Classic Library Series Offers Timeless Titles of Spiritual Renewal

Every book in this series has earned the "classic" status due to its popularity, durability, and uncompromising quality. Each brings a special viewpoint and understanding of the beliefs and principles of Unity. Each book is a respected addition to any metaphysical collection.

H. EMILIE CADY
Lessons in Truth

CHARLES FILLMORE
Atom-Smashing Power of Mind
Jesus Christ Heals
Keep a True Lent
Mysteries of Genesis
Mysteries of John
Prosperity
Talks on Truth

CHARLES AND CORA FILLMORE
Teach Us to Pray
The Twelve Powers

LOWELL FILLMORE
The Prayer Way to Health, Wealth, and Happiness

MYRTLE FILLMORE
How to Let God Help You

FRANCES W. FOULKS
Effectual Prayer

IMELDA SHANKLIN
What Are You?

ELIZABETH SAND TURNER
Be Ye Transformed
Let There Be Light
Your Hope of Glory

GEORGIANA TREE WEST
Prosperity's Ten Commandments

ERNEST C. WILSON
The Week That Changed the World

199-11288-250-11-05 Q